GOOGLE APPS MADE EASY

A complete guide that will teach you how to make the best use of Google apps and services in less than 7 days. Includes How to Use Google Classroom.

TIM TURNER

FOUDER OF DATA INTELLIGENCE AND TECH ACADEMY

Table of Contents

Introduction

The focus of this book is to explain what Google Apps are and how to use specific apps that suit your needs. The goal is not to make you a Google Apps expert, but rather to get to the point where you are proficient with the applications and can work on becoming an expert. Not everyone will need all of the apps that Google provides, but the goal is to inform you about the available apps so you can choose which ones will work for you.

Google has been providing apps for many years now and keeps adding more and more as time goes on. They even have their G Suite that you can subscribe to if you want to take your app usage to the next level at the workplace, but for most home users and even small business owners, the free apps should do the job just fine.

Google Apps involves no software installation whatsoever and no additional server hardware or infrastructure. Remember that cloud services are independent of the users' computer, run in a browser, and download themselves on-demand and invisibly to the user. This means the days of corrupted installations and missing software are over. Google Apps empowers you to distribute an entire productivity suite to up to 50 users without purchasing anything.

Business organizations, instructional establishments, and even humans can use the Google Apps provider for free. And due to the fact Google Apps require little or no technical expertise, it can also be a blessing for small commercial enterprise proprietors who have little or no price range for IT.

You will find that many of these apps are integrated with other apps and other Google services. This is done so you can seamlessly go from one app to another without having to wonder where your data is or figure out how to tie everything together manually. Many of the apps have similar features as well, so once you learn how to use one efficiently, there's a good chance that knowledge will transfer over to other apps.

A range of factors of Google Apps (like calendar, e-mail, spreadsheet, phrase processor, etc.) are hosted on Google servers, and so the quit customers are saved from the hassles of putting in or upgrading software program at their end. Administrators can get entry to and control person bills even though a web-based manipulate panel. The digital collaboration points of Google Docs are some distance greatest and effortless than what is presently presented via Microsoft Office applications.

If you plan to use a current internet area with Google Apps, simply make positive that you have to get entry to your DNS settings, which is usually reachable with the area host.

Google Apps is handy in two flavors – the well-known (aka free) version and a premier (aka paid) edition. The premier version subscribers are given 10GB of e-mail storage house (as hostile to

2GB+ in the free edition) and a 99.9% uptime assurance for e-mail.

Other top-class amenities encompass getting entry to 24/7 to assist via phone, covering all contextual classified ads on Google offerings, and numerous superior aspects tailor-made for the enterprise.

The premier version doesn't come low cost — it charges a whopping $50 per consumer account per yrs. - however, the desirable information is that most families, enterprise proprietors, and persons will be pretty content material with the choices of the well-known version because, besides phone guides and small inboxes, Google is supplying the identical functions in each the editions.

Chapter 1: Introducing google app

What are Google Apps?

Google Apps is a term used to describe the group of web-based applications provided by Google that you can use for a variety of things such as email, creating documents, calendars, note-taking, file storage and sharing, and so on. Most of these apps are free to use, and once you have a Google account, you automatically have access to start using these apps.

Since they are web-based and platform-independent, you can run them on almost any device from your Windows PC, MacBook, Android smartphone, iPhone, iPad, and many other devices. One thing you will need is an Internet connection, since most of the things you will do with these apps are "cloud-based" and done online.

One of the best things about these apps being run in the cloud and having the ability to also store your files in the cloud is that it makes it easier to share your files and your work with others, which makes collaboration much easier. There's no need to email attachments back and forth and copy files to flash drives because everything is stored online, and it's just a matter of allowing others access to your data so they can participate in the work process.

Why they are so convenient and their benefits.

Google is a solid trendsetter in the specialized administration industry. Over ten years prior, they spearheaded requests in the enormous confusion of data that made up the Internet. Today the turmoil develops, but they keep on having the option to support demand in their hunt administration. It's no big surprise that they would, in the long run, branch out to handle the confusion that exists for getting organizations associated with the data they have to remain on top of their staff and clients.

Accommodation of Remaining Associated

It has become standard for many businesses to work permanently and in the cloud. Email, archive sharing, and visit carry that administration to even the littlest business, which is an enormous advance up from the times of sending documents and sorting out telephone calls as the primary methods for remaining associated. So far, in my current utilization of the framework, it's been straightforward to: make a report and offer it, video, or message immediately with somebody without going through the motions. Available.

No upgrades ever needed

Software upgrades are a major headache for IT groups, especially in larger organizations – as users grow in number, the complexity grows exponentially. Types of the operating system, hardware, custom user configurations, and system availability are all barriers to providing users with the latest version, which is why most software vendors provide major upgrades infrequently.

With Google Apps, upgrades are no longer a project in themselves since they happen constantly and automatically. All your users receive the latest versions with no interruption in service and without IT staff having to work during weekends and other periods when users will not be impacted.

Increased reliability

'Uptime' refers to the percentage of time that a machine or service is usable. When an Exchange server or file server fails in your company, it has the capability of denying service to everyone since it can be the single point of failure. Google Apps boasts at the uptime of 99.9% (which means the system may be unavailable for up to 9 hours a year).

Increased security

Data backups are usually made on a schedule - monthly, weekly, or daily - but not instantaneously, so even with a good backup strategy, it's possible to lose data between backups if a version of a file is deleted or unintentionally modified. Google Apps backs up the entire revision history of every document in real-time in multiple locations – on-site backup will simply never be this good. Furthermore, there is no data physically stored at your site, so if computers are lost or stolen, or hard disks crash, your data is still safe (and inaccessible to third parties, in the case of hardware theft).

Great support

Most desktop software support doesn't compare to the breadth and depth of support data at Google. There are forums, discussion boards, help centers – all maintained and updated constantly. For Premier and educational users, email and phone assistance are available 24/7, which is not common in the world of desktop software.

It's also worth mentioning that pushing applications into the cloud reduces complexity on your side and helps reduce the need for support in the first place. The vast majority of helpdesk issues are related to a specific machine or software installation, and many of these disappear when there's nothing locally installed.

World-class collaboration

Collaboration has never really worked in traditional software because it involves emailing files or synchronizing groups of people, and it's hard to see what other users are working on. Google Apps takes a much simpler approach and enables users to see changes in real-time. Literally, content changes before your eyes when another user is editing the same document. After five minutes of working on a spreadsheet with a colleague across the country, it's clear to see why this is so powerful and how multiple out-of-sync versions simply don't exist anymore.

Unwavering Quality in a very much Perceived Brand

The advantages of unwavering quality originate from the diminished multifaceted nature that would regularly be related to any of the above administrations. This qualification as a Google administration is significant because the brand has gotten very much perceived for its unwavering quality in the administrations it gives.

Productivity with High Esteemed Assignments

The client experience is natural for any event the usefulness that is utilized for a business, which implies practically zero preparing for their representatives. Since it's on the cloud, there is no requirement for programming updates to be introduced routinely. It's likewise packaged with their quick pursuit device to discover things rapidly and effectively yet not be secured by the tumult of developing data. This outcome in expanded profitability and a more joyful working environment since it's no pleasant battling innovation to complete things.

Administering Google Apps is Simple

The administrator interface is dead-easy to utilize and simple. All that you need to control for your space has a catch or switch in the back end.

The Admin Control Panel makes it far simpler to explore essential administrator capacities than any Microsoft server programming. You can include erase or suspend clients, move responsibility for archives, make nom de plumes, and change the least secret phrase necessities.

Signing up for a Google Account

The first thing you need to do before being able to use all of these apps is to sign up for a Google account. Since all of these apps will be tied to **you** specifically, it's necessary to have a way to log in, so you have all of the information that belongs to you each time you use an app. Simply enter your first and last name and choose a username, which will also be used for your Gmail email account ending in @gmail.com. If the username has already been taken, then you will be prompted to enter a new one. Notice that there is an option that says **Use my current email address instead**. This can be done if you do not want a Gmail email address, but still want to create a Google account with your current email address.

 Next, you enter a recovery email address (which can also be used for password recovery), as well as your birth date information. The birth date information is used because some Google services have age requirements. The gender information it asks for is optional and is not shown to other Google users. You can also edit your Google account later if you wish to change or add anything.

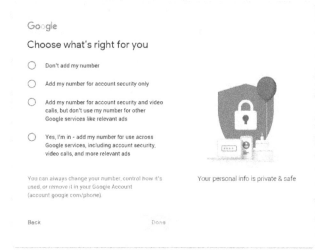

Google

Choose what's right for you

○ Don't add my number

○ Add my number for account security only

○ Add my number for account security and video calls, but don't use my number for other Google services like relevant ads

○ Yes, I'm in - add my number for use across Google services, including account security, video calls, and more relevant ads

You can always change your number, control how it's used, or remove it in your Google Account (account.google.com/phone).

Your personal info is private & safe

Back   Done

If you are on the Google home page, then you will see your first initial up in the right-hand corner. You can go into your settings and edit your profile and add a picture if you like.

Account Settings

Before you get too involved in using your new Google Apps, you might want to take a look at your Google settings to make sure all of the security and privacy settings are set the way you like. To get to your settings, click on the circle with your initials in it on the top right of the screen on the Google homepage (www.google.com), and then click on the **Google Account** button.

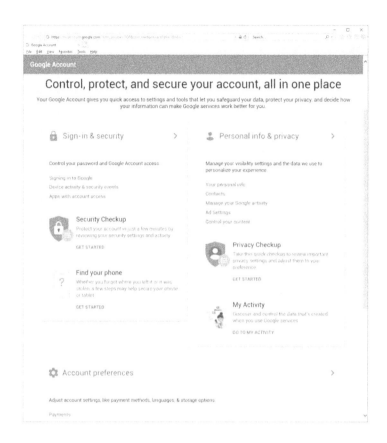

Search and install your google apps.

Now that you are signed up with your new Google account (assuming you didn't already have one), you might be wondering how to find the apps that you plan on using or even the ones you want to try out before deciding if they are right for you or not.

There are several ways to go about finding and opening your Google Apps, but if you are on the Google homepage, then all you need to do is click on the icon that consists of nine small boxes to bring up many of the Google Apps

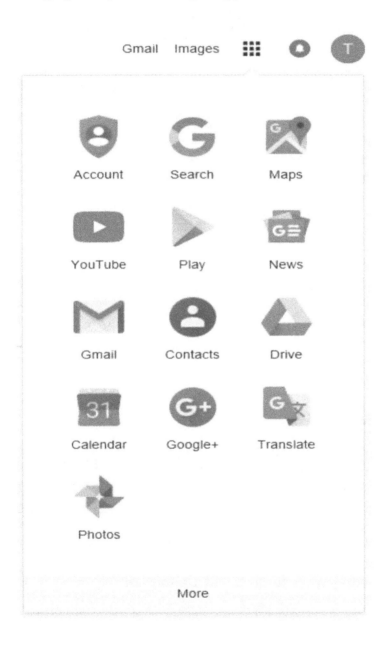

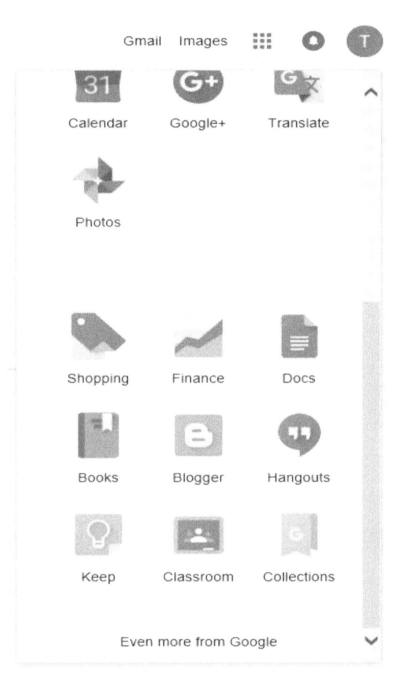

If you **still** can't find what you're looking for, you can simply do a Google search for that app and then open it from the search results. Once you figure out what apps you will be using, it might be a good idea to make bookmarks for each one and then make a bookmark folder to put them in, so they are all in one place.

Chapter 2: Google drive

Google gives its members free online storage space that is kept "in the cloud" (meaning it can be accessed from just about anywhere). You can also use it to share files with other people.

Getting started to Google Drive:

There can be many different methods to access Google Drive, out of which the easiest is to use a Chrome browser. After clicking Chrome, click on a browser or on the new tab. Here you will find the page shown below. Just select the logo for Google Drive, which will direct you to the website for Google Drive.

In case one does not have the Chrome browser, then adding the appropriate URL in the search bar will also direct the user to get access to Google Drive, as shown below:

3. There can be another method for accessing Google Drive: search for Google Drive on Google.

Interface of Google Drive:

The Google Drive entails the following interface: The "My Drive" is actually in synchronization with the desktop of the user.

All of the folders appearing under My Drive will be similar to the ones which are within the desktop. You can use the Drag Drop function to put any of the files from the internet to "My Drive".

Desktop Application for Google Drive

When the initial login for Google Drive is made, it will prompt the user to download the application for the desktop. You will need to click on the Download option.

Next, click "Accept and Install"

 Next, click on the "Save File" icon for opening the download and proceed to "Run". It will automatically administer you to the necessary steps for downloading.

After downloading the Drive, the next step is to get signed in with a Google account. To start the synchronization of Google Documents with Google drive, click to "Start Sync".

After this step, Google Drive will be one of the options for saving the files. You will get a shortcut for Drive over the desktop. You can also apply a Drag- Drop function to directly add files to the drive for the internet or some other source.

Google Drive over the Web

There is an arrow on the left side of "My Drive", which is used to expand the Drive and show all the folders which have been synchronized with the Google Drive. Select any of the folders, and its content will be displayed at the right of the screen.

In case you add some folder or file over the desktop, it will automatically become part of the Drive.

Adding to folders in the "My Drive" is also possible. First of all, click "Create "and from the drop-down options and select the "Folders" options.

Give a name to the new folder, and it will become part of my drive folders, just like the previous ones.

Synchronization and file sharing

One of the most celebrated features of Google Drive is its ability to serve as a backup for all types of files. In this case, the desktop sync utility of Google will be used, which adds a specific folder to the system's hard drive, which then acts as a two-way channel.

 Carrying out the backup function with Google drive is a simple process which is executed with three simple steps:

This first step will relate to the primary step of Downloading and install the Google Drive utility. This is available for both Windows as well as for Mac. However, the basic working and sequence of steps will be the same in both cases.

The next step will be to run the program over the system. Now sign in with your Google account. Here the screen will guide you through the step by step procedure.

The initial few steps may be for informative purposes only where you will get guidance for using the tool. The next steps will carry you on with the actual procedure. At the last step, click "Done" or "Finish".

As the last step, Google Drive will open directly in the Explorer window, enabling you to scrutinize all the documents which are currently available in the document. Now this folder will be available on the hard disk of the system and at the Google drive as well.

This utility of Google Drive has enabled a safe and secure environment for the user in which the user no longer worries about the file storage or a system getting corrupted. As it will be available at both places, so enhanced comfort has been added by Google Drive.

Creating folder and uploading files;

Creating Folders and Uploading Files

It's very easy to create a new folder in Google Drive. All you need to do is click right on the location where you want to create your folder (such as My Drive), choose **New Folder**, and give it a name. Then you can go into that folder and upload some files. To do so, simply right-click on a blank area and choose **Upload files,** or you can actually drag and drop the files from your computer right into your web browser.

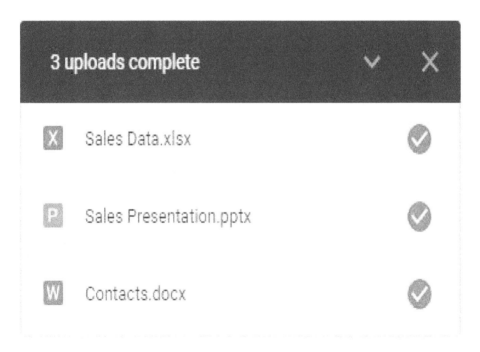

Then, when you are back at that folder, you will see your newly added files (as shown below)

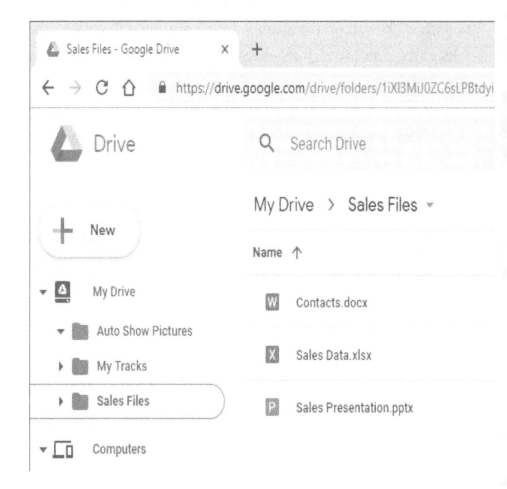

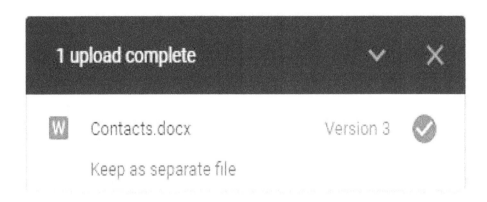

You can upload as many files as you have room for. You can also upload folders using the same methods that you can use for uploading files.

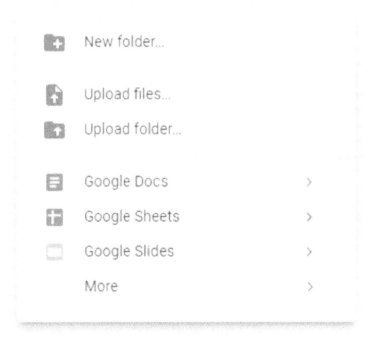

You might have noticed while you were right-clicking that there are options for things like Google Docs and Google Sheets This is because Google wants you to use its Google Docs service, which is similar to Microsoft's Office 365, and allows you to use things like a word processor and spreadsheet app online rather than having to install one on your computer

Managing Files and Folders

Once you get your folders created and files uploaded, you will need to know how to manage them, so you know where things are, and so your storage doesn't turn into a mess of unmanageable files.

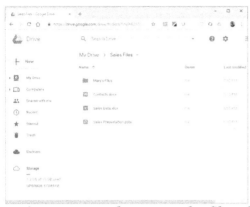

Let's say we need to move the file called **Contacts.docx** to a new folder for a user called Mary. The first thing to do is right-click on a blank spot within the Sales Files folder and choose **New folder**. Then let's call it **Mary's Files** and click on **Create**.

Now, as you can see in, we have a folder called **Mary's Files**, and we just need to move the Contacts.docx file into that folder. There are a couple of ways we can this.

One way is to the right-click the Contacts.docx file, choose **Move to**, and then choose the **Mary's Files** folder, which will get it moved into that folder.

An easier way to do this is to just click on the **Contacts.docx** file and drag it into the **Mary's Files** folder. Either way, you will get a message similar to figure 2.8, telling you what happened.

If you were then to go into the **Mary's Files** folder, you would find that the **Contacts.docx** file is now located in that folder.

Here is what each of the right-click options will do to your file:

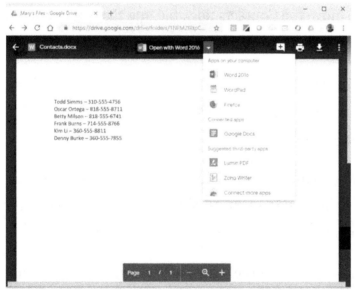

Google Drive will also suggest other methods of opening your file based on the type of file. You can see that it suggested opening the file using Word 2016, and if you click the dropdown arrow next to that, there will be other options such as WordPad and Google Docs, which you can try if the preview function doesn't work.

Open with – This will give you choices of programs to open the file with

Share – This allows you to share your file with other people via a link or an email invite.

Get sharable link – The same thing applies about sharing for this option, but what this does is create a link to your shared file that people can click on to have access to your file.

Add star – If you want a particular file to stand out, then you can add a star to it (figure 2.11), which will remind you that there is something special about it. There is also a Starred section in the main OneDrive area where you can view all of your starred files in one place.

Rename — This is pretty self-explanatory, but one thing you need to keep in mind is that if you change the file extension (in this case it's .docx), then you might not be able to open the file anymore since Windows (and Mac\Linux) use file extensions to tell the operating system what program it should open the file with.

View details — Here, you can view the details and activity of a certain file. As you can see in, there is a Details section and an Activity section, and each one shows different information about the file, such as its size, location, owner, as well as edit and move activity (etc.).

Manage versions – If you have multiple versions of a file that you have either changed and saved or uploaded a new copy and overwritten the existing copy, then you will have some options as to what you can do with those various versions (figure 2.13). Google will keep your older versions for thirty days (or 100 versions) before removing them, so if you need to go back to an older version, you will be able to do so. Then you can click on the three dots menu to either download the file, delete the file, or have Google keep the file forever.

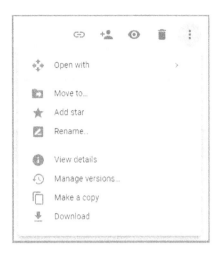

Make a copy – This option will simply create a copy of the file and place it in the same folder with the same name, except it will say **"Copy of"** in front of it.

Download – If you want to have a copy of this file on your local computer, then choose this option and select the folder on your hard drive where you want to download the file to.

Remove – This option will remove the file from your Google Drive and place it the Trash, where you can go and restore the file if needed. To do so, just right-click the file in the Trash and choose **Restore**. Or you can choose to **Delete forever** to permanently remove it

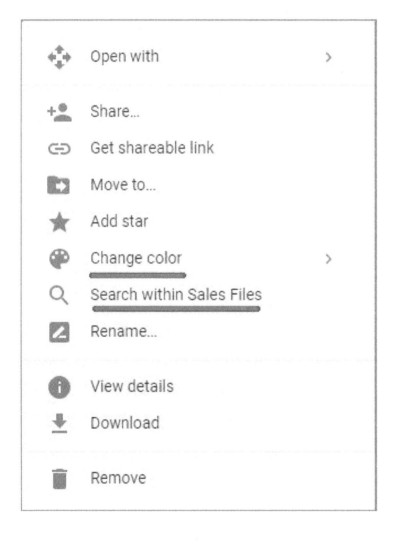

The **Change color** choice will change the color of the folder from the default grey to whatever color you like.

 The **Search within** choice will let you search for files within the folder you right-clicked on. You can search by name and also by file type.

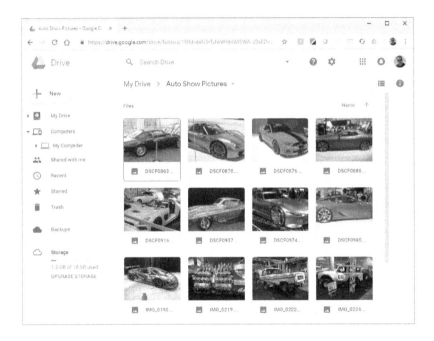

Chapter 3: Google docs

Docs – This is Google's word processor program, similar to Microsoft Word. You can use it to create things like letters, resumes, lists, and so on.

This is Google's word processor program, similar to Microsoft Word. You can use it to create things like letters, resumes, lists, and so on.

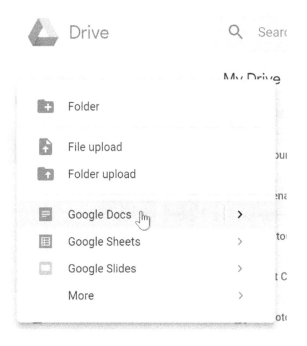

The entire Google Apps appears to turn to gold. No longer handiest has the brand helped online groups generate billions of greenbacks via its search engine, but it is also — and maintains —

department out and create other merchandise. One of the products is google docs, a loose word-processor and opportunity to Microsoft office that allows all the apps to create and edit their shareable file.

Signing Up for an Account

Go to www. Google. Com. Find and select the check-in button within the top-right nook of the web page. Sign up button. Click on create an account. Create an account link. The sign-up shape will appear. Comply with the directions and enter the desired statistics. Join up form. Next, input your cellphone range. Google will ship a verification code for your telephone that you may use to complete the sign-up method. Enter telephone quantity. Input the verification code sent for your cellphone and click on verify. Affirm smartphone quantity with the system.

Creating and sharing a text document.

Google Power gives you access to a set of devices that allow you to create and edit a wide range of files, including documents, spreadsheets, and displays. There are five styles of documents you may create on google power:

Documents

Composing letters, flyers, essays, and different text-based files (just like Microsoft Word files)

Spreadsheets

For storing and organizing data (similar to Microsoft Excel workbooks)

Displays

For growing slideshows (just like Microsoft PowerPoint shows)

Bureaucracy

For gathering and organizing information drawings: for creating easy vector pictures or diagrams,

The technique for creating new documents is the same for all document kinds. Watch the video underneath to analyze more. To create a new document:

Google power, discover and pick out the new button, and then pick the form of the file you want to create. In our instance, we'll choose google docs to create a new record. Selecting google docs from the menu, your new file will appear in a brand new tab in your browser. Find and select the untitled report within the top-left corner. Choosing untitled report. The rename conversation container will seem. Kind a name to your record, then click ok. Typing a new call. Your file will be renamed. You may access the file from your google drive at any time, in which it will likely be saved automatically.

Sincerely double-click to open the report again. Displaying document after renaming,

The Interfaces

Your google drive can be empty right now, but as you start to upload and create files, you will want to realize how to view, manipulate, and organize them in the interface. Click on the buttons in the interactive underneath to become acquainted with the google force interface. Google power cellular interface. Google additionally has separate mobile apps for creating and enhancing files, spreadsheets, and shows. To study higher, test out Google's blog, publish on new cell apps for doctors, sheets, and slides. Google power for a computing device

In case you prefer to paintings at the computing device, you can download the google force laptop app on your pc. To be had for windows and so x, this app makes it a bit simpler to upload your present documents and paintings offline. Once it is established, you will see a new google power folder for your pc. Any materials you move into this folder will routinely be uploaded for your google power.

Google Doc's Menu Settings

A pop-up field will then be seen on your display screen. To set up offline enhancing, toggle the offline button to on. (This needs to turn the button blue, instead of grey.)google docs offline toggle

Edit and Format a Document

Google docs empower you to create a report that works for you and the content material you're developing. Whether or not it's the web page orientation, pix, or web page numbers, those recommendations will help you layout your file any manner you need.

Changing Page Margins

Converting Page Orientation

Adding a Textual Content Container

Adding Page Numbers

Growing a Placing Indent

Putting a Picture

Growing a Table of Contents

Converting Web Page Margins

In case you're seeking to make the maximum of the clean area for your report or format your report for printing, you may need to change the margins. In advance of doing this, you will want to make sure the ruler is seen above your document. Surely head to view > display ruler.

Print and Download Documents

Once you've created a report, it will likely be accessible every time you check in to google drive. There might be times when you need to import or print a paper offline for entry.

To Download a Document

Find and right-click on the report you need to download, then pick download. The file could be downloaded on your pc. To select a file layout:

The article will appear in the new window. Choose description> download as, then select the favored file type. In this example, we'll pick the pdf document (. Pdf). The file could be downloaded in your pc within the favored document kind. To print conversation container will seem, alongside a preview of your file at the right. Pick out the desired alternatives, then click print. Be aware that those options will vary relying on the type of report you're printing. For example, you'll have different options for writing a spreadsheet then you'll for writing a presentation.

Publishing document

Now that you have your document completed and formatted the way you like, it's time to print it out on some paper, or maybe even publish it online, so others can view your work for themselves.

To print your document, go to the **File** menu and then to **Print,** and you will be shown a preview of how your document will print, and also have some choices to make before actually printing your document.

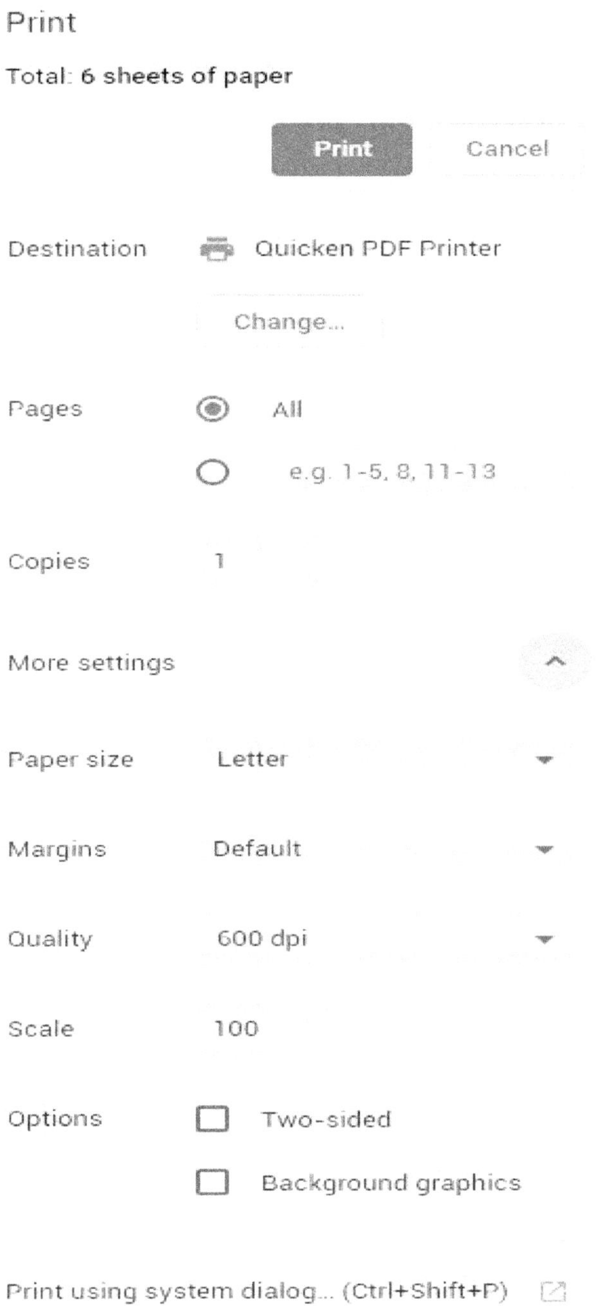

Print

Total: **6 sheets of paper**

Print	Cancel

Destination   🖶 Quicken PDF Printer

Change...

Pages   ⦿   All

            ○   e.g. 1-5, 8, 11-13

Copies   1

More settings   ⌃

Paper size   Letter   ▾

Margins   Default   ▾

Quality   600 dpi   ▾

Scale   100

Options   ☐   Two-sided

              ☐   Background graphics

Print using system dialog... (Ctrl+Shift+P)   ⬈

The **Destination** shows what printer the document will be sent to for printing, so if you need to change that to another printer or even a PDF printer, you can click on the **Change** button.

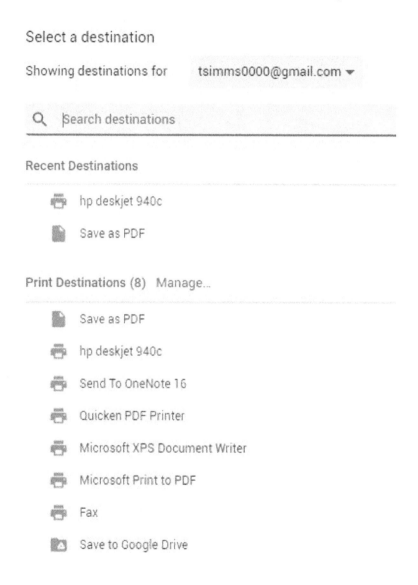

Select a destination

Showing destinations for   tsimms0000@gmail.com ▾

Q Search destinations

Recent Destinations

🖨 hp deskjet 940c

📄 Save as PDF

Print Destinations (8)   Manage...

📄 Save as PDF

🖨 hp deskjet 940c

🖨 Send To OneNote 16

🖨 Quicken PDF Printer

🖨 Microsoft XPS Document Writer

🖨 Microsoft Print to PDF

🖨 Fax

📇 Save to Google Drive

By default, Docs will want to print the entire document, but you can change that by clicking the radio button under **Pages** to the second one and adding the pages you want to print. So, if you wanted to only print pages 1 through 3, you would enter **1-3** in the box. If you wanted to print pages 1,3, and 5, you would enter **1,3,5** in the box.

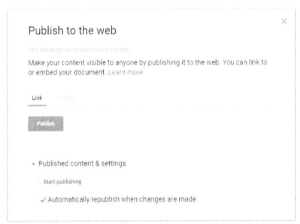

More settings, which can be accessed by clicking the down arrow next to it, there will be some additional formatting options that you can apply to your document before printing it. Here you can change the **paper size** to one of the included sizes, as well as enter in a custom page size of your own. You can also change the **margins** if they need to be adjusted to make things look correct on the page when printed. The default dpi (dots per inch) next to **Quality** is 600, which should be plenty for most print jobs (unless you are printing super high-resolution pictures and your printer can actually **do** so).

Publishing a Document

Link – Using this option will publish your document to the Internet, where others with the link will be able to view it. They will not be able to edit it or do anything else with it except print it. Once you click on **Publish,** it will publish your document and give you a link

Then you can share that link via services such as Google+, Gmail, Facebook, and Twitter, or copy the link and email it to someone else so they can view your document.

Embed – Choosing this option will get you the HTML code that you can use to embed your document into an existing webpage. A common example of embedding code is when someone places someone else's YouTube video on their website. This is done by embedding the code linked to that video.

Once you click on **Start publishing,** you will be presented with the HTML code required to embed your document onto your website.

Sharing a Document

Sharing a document is similar to publishing a document with the main difference being that it's actually opened with Google Docs, and you can give other people the right to edit your document. The sharing process works the same for other Google apps like Sheets and Slides.

You can share your document by clicking the **Share** button next to your profile picture on the top right of the screen.

By default, your document is set to private, so only you can access it, but it's easy to give others permission to view and even edit your document by clicking on **Change**.

There are three options you can set for link sharing: On (public on the web) – This will make your document public on the Internet and allow anyone to find it by searching for items contained in it. If you choose this option, you can set the permissions to be view only, comment, or edit.

When you invite a person who doesn't have a Google account, you will need to make a choice between **Send an invitation** or **Send the link**If the person you are sending the invitation to will need to edit the document. They will need to sign in with a Google account.

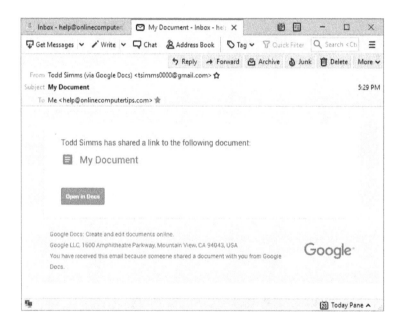

If they just need to view the document, then they can do so by clicking on the link they receive in the email that will be sent to them.

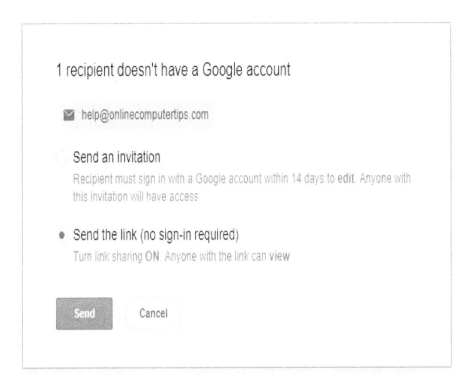

1 recipient doesn't have a Google account

✉ help@onlinecomputertips.com

○ Send an invitation
Recipient must sign in with a Google account within 14 days to edit. Anyone with this invitation will have access

● Send the link (no sign-in required)
Turn link sharing ON. Anyone with the link can view

Send   Cancel

Once you share your document with a non-Google user, you should see a new icon on your toolbar next to the Share button. (It's usually some random animal showing you that an anonymous user is accessing your document.)

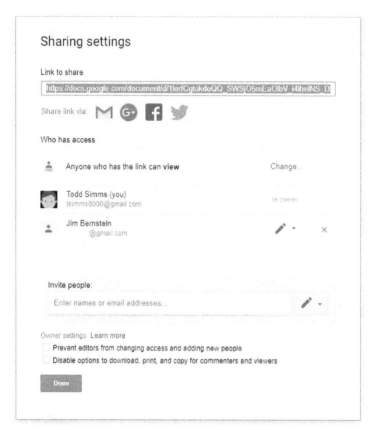

Sharing settings

Link to share

https://docs.google.com/document/d/1IorICgtokdoQQ_SWSjO5mEaOlbV-i4IheINS_D

Share link via: M G+ f y

Who has access

Anyone who has the link can view   Change...

Todd Simms (you)
tsimms0000@gmail.com   is owner

Jim Bernstein
@gmail.com   ✏ ▾   ×

Invite people:

Enter names or email addresses...   ✏ ▾

Owner settings Learn more
☐ Prevent editors from changing access and adding new people
☐ Disable options to download, print, and copy for commenters and viewers

Done

If you don't want anyone that you have assigned the editor right to change your sharing access or add other people without your permission, then you can check the box that says **Prevent editors from changing access and adding new people**.

Chapter 4: Google Sheets

This is Google's spreadsheet program, similar to Microsoft Excel. It has a similar look and feels to Excel as well.

Connect spreadsheets, one of the motives that have seen people resistant to the usage of google sheets, is because they think certain functions from excel are missing. In truth, the maximum of those capabilities are already applied in sheets— you simply ought to realize in which to move searching out them. A traditional instance of this is the ability to grab statistics from different spreadsheets. The use of functions like =import range makes it possible to go and get statistics from absolutely separate workbooks. Ensure to read the academic below to stroll via the usage of a couple of spreadsheets in sync and pull data to and fro. Three. Examine even as you operate the product. While they are easy to get commenced with, it's the formulas and features that can sense like plenty to learn.

Creating a Spreadsheet

Cell: A single statistics point or element in a spreadsheet.

Column: A vertical set of batteries.

Row: A horizontal set of batteries.

Range: A spread of cells extending throughout a row, column, or each.

The first-rate element about google sheets is that it is unfastened and works on any device—which makes it clean to follow alongside the tutorials on this e-book. All you'll want is an internet browser (or the google sheets app in your IOS or android tool) and an unfastened google account. To your mac or computer, head over to sheets. Google. You and Corer are equipped to get commenced.

There is three-course of action to create a new spreadsheet in google sheets:

1.   Press enter to keep the records and circulate to the start of the next row

2.   Press tab to keep the facts and flow to the right inside the same row

3.   Use the arrow keys to your keyboard (up, down, left, and proper) to move one cell in that direction

4.   Click any mobile to leap without delay to that cellular

If you don't want to kind in the whole thing manually; you may additionally upload statistics for your sheet and masse through a few different techniques:

1. Copy and paste a list of documents or numbers into your spreadsheet

2. Copy and paste an HTML writing table from a website

3. Import an existing worksheet in CSV, Xls, xlsx and other codecs

4. Replica any cost in a cell across a variety of cells via a click on and drag

Sheet interface;

Google sheets accessories google has taken a quite open approach to develop sheets, welcoming accessories from different developers to decorate what sheets can do natively. think about accessories in two essential categories:

Description of all menu; Creating a spreadsheet;

Formatting a spreadsheet;

Performing calculation and using formulas;

Formatting a Spreadsheet

There are many ways to format your spreadsheet, and how you do it is completely up to you. Just keep in mind that if other people are viewing or using your spreadsheet, you will want to keep your formatting subtle so they can do what they need to do and not be distracted by neon colors and hard to read fonts.

	Cathy	Joe	Lisa	Maria	Steve	Allen
Monday	7	8	9	6	8	6
Tuesday	8	0	4	0	8	5
Wednesday	5	9	5	7	6	3
Thursday	6	5	8	7	9	6
Friday	9	6	8	0	7	7
Saturday	3	0	2	0	5	0
Sunday	0	2	2	0	0	3

Next, go up to the toolbar and find the **Borders** button and click on it to see my available border choices. There are several default styles you can use, which will be black in color, or you can change the border to any color you like and even change the line type to something like dashed or dotted.

E	F	G
	Steve	Allen
6	8	6
8	8	5
7	8	3
7	9	5
8	7	7
0	5	0
0	0	3

	A	B Cathy	C Joe	D Lisa	E Maria	F Steve	G Allen
1		Cathy	Joe	Lisa	Maria	Steve	Allen
2	Monday	7	8	9	6	8	6
3	Tuesday	8	8	4	8	8	5
4	Wednesday	5	9	5	7	8	3
5	Thursday	6	5	8	7	9	5
6	Friday	9	6	8	8	7	7
7	Saturday	3	0	2	0	5	0
8	Sunday	0	2	2	0	0	3
9							
10							

61

	A	Cathy	Joe	Lisa	Maria	Steve	Allen
1		Cathy	Joe	Lisa	Maria	Steve	Allen
2	Monday	7	8	9	6	8	6
3	Tuesday	8	8	4	8	8	5
4	Wednesday	5	9	5	7	8	3
5	Thursday	6	5	8	7	9	5
6	Friday	9	6	8	8	7	7
7	Saturday	3	0	2	0	5	0
8	Sunday	0	2	2	0	0	3
9							

For the days of the week, I want to have them use alternating colors, so it's easier to look down each row and keep track of what day we are on. For this, I will highlight the range of A1 through G8, go to the Format menu, choose **Alternating colors** (discussed earlier), and will choose the orange theme for this example.

	A	B	C	D	E	F	G
1		Cathy	Joe	Lisa	Maria	Steve	Allen
2	Monday	7	8	9	6	8	6
3	Tuesday	8	8	4	8	8	5
4	Wednesday	5	9	5	7	8	3
5	Thursday	6	5	8	7	9	5
6	Friday	9	6	8	8	7	7
7	Saturday	3	0	2	0	5	0
8	Sunday	0	2	2	0	0	3

The first way involves highlighting the entire table and dragging it down a row so the name Cathy will be in cell B2 and so on. Once the range is highlighted, place your cursor on the edge of the highlighted range until it turns into a hand, and then click and hold while dragging the table down to the next row. Then you can release the mouse button.

D	E	F	G
Lisa	Maria	Steve	Allen
9	6	8	6
4	8	8	5
5	7	8	3
8	7	9	5
8	8	7	7
2	0	5	0
2	0	0	3

Figure 4.88

An easier way to do this would be to right-click on the row number you want to add a row above (in this case row 1) and then choose **Insert 1 above**. If you are following along, you might have noticed that the alternating colors stayed at row 1 instead of moving down to row 2.

	A	B	C	D	E	F	G
1							
2		Cathy	Joe	Lisa	Maria	Steve	Allen
3	Monday	7	8	9	6	8	6
4	Tuesday	8	8	4	8	8	5
5	Wednesday	5	9	5	7	8	3
6	Thursday	6	5	8	7	9	5
7	Friday	9	6	8	8	7	7
8	Saturday	3	0	2	0	5	0
9	Sunday	0	2	2	0	0	3
10							

100% ▾ $ % .0 .00 123▾ Arial ▾ 18 ▾ B I S A ◆. ⊞ ⊞▾ ≡▾ ⊥▾ ⊬▾ ⯈

Empoyee Hours

Merge all

Merge horizontally

Merge vertically

Unmerge

	A	B	C	D	E	F	G
1	Empoyee Hours						
2		Cathy	Joe	Lisa	Maria	Steve	Allen
3	Monday	7	8	9	6	8	
4	Tuesday	8	8	4	8	8	5
5	Wednesday	5	9	5	7	8	3
6	Thursday	6	5	8	7	9	5
7	Friday	9	6	8	8	7	7
8	Saturday	3	0	2	0	5	0
9	Sunday	0	2	2	0	0	3
10							

	Cathy	Joe	Lisa	Maria	Steve	Allen
Empoyee Hours						
Monday	7	8	9	6	8	6
Tuesday	8	8	4	8	8	5
Wednesday	5	9	5	7	8	3
Thursday	6	5	8	7	9	5
Friday	9	6	8	8	7	7
Saturday	3	0	2	0	5	0
Sunday	0	2	2	0	0	3

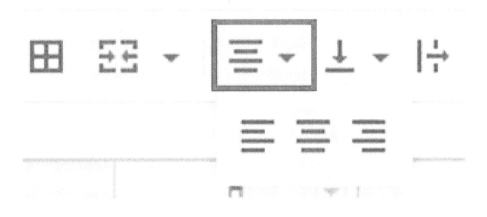

	Cathy	Joe	Lisa	Maria	Steve	Allen
			Empoyee Hours			
Monday	7	8	9	6	8	6
Tuesday	8	8	4	8	8	5
Wednesday	5	9	5	7	8	3
Thursday	6	5	8	7	9	5
Friday	9	6	8	8	7	7
Saturday	3	0	2	0	5	0
Sunday	0	2	2	0	0	3

Unlike other spreadsheet software, Google Sheets has many built-in methods for executing a variety of mathematical and data processing activities. You may also merge formulas to allow more dynamic equations and add activities together. And if you're still used to crunching numbers in Excel, the same calculations function much of the time in Google Pages.

Using the Sum Method

Allows begin with including up the entire wide variety of ingredients required for every recipe. I'll use the sum formula to add each cost within the recipes and get a total quantity. There are three methods to use the simple formulas accessible thru the pinnacle navigation:

1. Select a range then click on the system (this may position the result both under and to the aspect of the field).

2. Select the resulting mobile (i.e., the cellular where you want the result to seem), then click at the method you need to use from the toolbar.

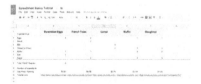

Notice: for you to pick out quite several cells, click on the primary cellular and maintain shift, then click on the last mobile within the variety. So if you want a1 thru a10, click on a1 then preserve shift and click a10. While you've finished choosing the cells which you wish to feature together, press input. In an example, you notice a gray assist section pop up once you begin typing the components. When you create a method for the first time, you'll, as a substitute, be aware of a blue spotlight and a query mark after the mobile. You could click on the query mark to toggle assist context for formulation on or off.

The use of the average formula

Now that we recognize how many components are wished for each calculation recognize how complicated it is to make. It is simplified via assuming that fewer components approach that the recipe is less complicated. To remember the number of ingredients in each component, you'll use the count components. They depend on formulation tests to peer if the cells in a selection are empty or now not and return the whole stuffed. This method could be an installation in your spreadsheet in the same manner as the sum row. If you've highlighted a pure list of numbers, sheets will robotically sum them for you and show the result. In case you've highlighted a combined variety of numbers and text, it will count the values

Formulation

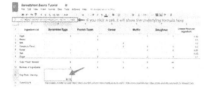

If we want to calculate the full price of the breakfast by multiplying the average charge of every element by using its unit matter in the recipe. To perform this, manually type a system into the "average fee" row. Our fundamental mathematics system could appear to be this for the "scrambled eggs" column:

=$i2*b2+$i3*b3+$i4*b4+$i5*b5+$i6*b6+$i7*b7+$i8*b8

In case you do not need to kind those values manually, there are cleanser ways to perform this form of the system: you could accomplish the same rate calculation by using this superior formulation:

=sum (array formula (b2:b8*$i2:$i8))

Creating a Chart

Now that we have some data, let's make a chart from it so we can see it in more of a top-down graphical view. Charts can be created from the **Insert** menu, and then by choosing **Chart**. What you will see here will vary on your data and if you are on that data when you click on the Chart option from the Insert menu.

The Setup options allow you to change various configurations of the chart, such as the chart type and data range. As you can see in figure 4.105, there are many types of charts to choose from.

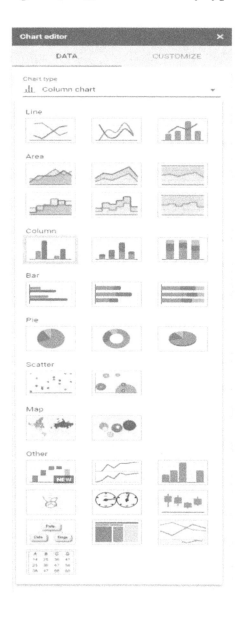

The **Data range** is what you need to focus on to get the right information into your chart. The easiest way to get the data range is to highlight the cells with the information that you want in your chart and Sheets will add it to the **What data** box or you can just click on one of the cells and let Sheets choose the data for you and see if it selects what you like.

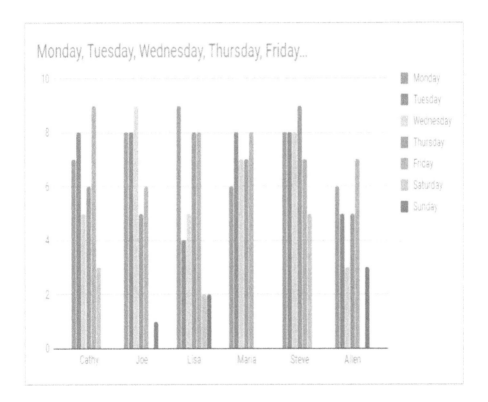

The **customize** section is where you can apply formatting options to your chart

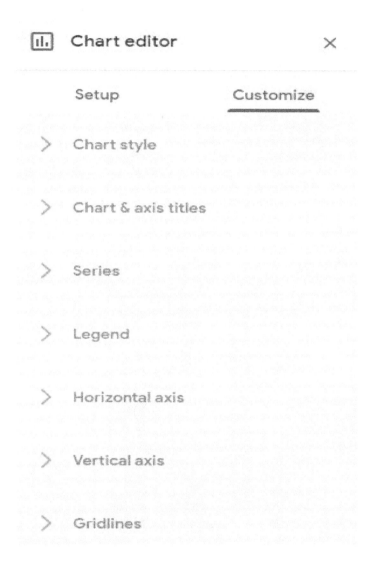

Here is a brief rundown of what each customization option will do

Chart style – Here, you can change things like the background color and chart font, as well as make your chart 3D or have it use compare mode if applicable. Chart & axis titles – In this section, you can do things like add a chart name and change the colors and fonts again. I will call my chart "Hours worked per employee" and center the title on the chart.

Series – The **Series** section will let you apply things such as data labels and trendline bars to your chart. Trendlines are lines across the chart that will show increases and decreases in the data

Legend – Here is where you can customize your legend labels in regards to position, font, and format.

Horizontal axis – If you need to change the formatting of the labels on the horizontal axis, you can do that here

Vertical axis – You can apply the same type of formatting here that you did for the horizontal axis.

Gridlines – Gridlines can be added to the horizontal and\or vertical axis to make things easier to read.

Sheets will place the chart inside of your spreadsheet, but you have the option to move it to its own sheet if you like by clicking on the three vertical dots at the top right of the chart and choosing

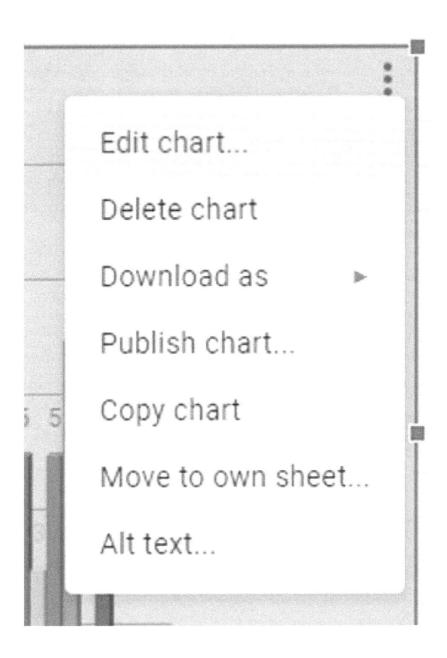

You can also do things such as download the chart as an image or PDF file and even publish it to the Internet for others to view. If you decide to publish your chart, it will work the same way as if you were publishing a document, where you will be given a link to that chart that you can send out to other people so they can view the chart.

Printing a Spreadsheet

Now that we have all the information in our chart, it's time to print it out so others can have their own copy (assuming you don't do the more common thing, which would be to email it).

Printing a spreadsheet is similar to printing a document, but there are some Sheet specific options that you can choose from when printing. You have the choice to print the current sheet that you are on, or you can also choose to only print cells that you have highlighted, or the entire spreadsheet (workbook) if you have more than one sheet.

Print
Current sheet ▾

Paper size
Letter (8.5" x 11") ▾

Page orientation
◉ Landscape   ◯ Portrait

Scale
Fit to page ▾

Margins
Normal ▾

SET CUSTOM PAGE BREAKS

Formatting ⌃

☑ Show gridlines

☑ Show notes

Page order
Over, then down ▾

Alignment

Horizontal   Vertical
Center ▾   Top ▾

Headers & footers ⌃

☐ Page numbers

☐ Workbook title

☐ Sheet name

☐ Current date

☐ Current time

EDIT CUSTOM FIELDS

Row & column headers

Go to View > Freeze to select which rows/columns to
repeat on all pages

☐ Repeat frozen rows

☐ Repeat frozen columns

Sheets will give you a print preview so you can see how your spreadsheet will look when printed. You might notice that your sheet doesn't fit correctly on one page and will be split into two separate pages for printing (figure 4.112). If that's the case, then you can go to the **Scale** section and choose to fit the page height or width or have it fit the page itself, which will make it smaller on the paper but make everything fit on one page.

Empoyee Hours

	Cathy	Joe	Lisa	Maria	Steve	Allen
Monday	7	8	9	6	8	6
Tuesday	8	8	4	8	8	5
Wednesday	5	9	5	7	8	3
Thursday	6	5	8	7	9	5
Friday	9	6	8	8	7	7
Saturday	3	0	2	0	5	0
Sunday	0	1	2	0	0	3
Totals	38	37	38	36	45	29
Average	5.43	5.29	5.43	5.14	6.43	4.14

Hours worked per employee

Under the **Formatting** section, you can choose whether or not to have gridlines or notes printed out with your spreadsheet. You can also change things such as the page order and alignment.

If you use any row or column headers that you have frozen to make things easier to read, then you can have those repeated on each page so that there is a header on every page. To freeze a row or column, all you need to is select the row or column, go to the **View** menu, and then click on **Freeze** and choose what you want to freeze.

	A	B	C	D	E	F	G
1		Empoyee Hours					
2		Cathy	Joe	Lisa	Maria	Steve	Allen
5	Wednesday	5	9	5	7	8	3
6	Thursday	6	5	8	7	9	5
7	Friday	9	6	8	8	7	7
8	Saturday	3	0	2	0	5	0
9	Sunday	0	1	2	0	0	3
10	Totals	38	37	38	36	45	29
11							
12	Average	5.43	5.29	5.43	5.14	6.43	4.14
13							

Chapter 5: Google slides

This is Google's presentation program, similar to Microsoft PowerPoint. It can be used to create slideshows and custom presentations that you can show during meetings and so on.

Slides interface

If you have ever used Microsoft PowerPoint to create presentations, then using Google Slides should be pretty easy to get the hang of. If you have **never** used presentation software, then you may still find Slides easy to use since there's not a whole lot to it (unless your plan is to get super fancy and make a big production out of your presentation).

Slides is basically an app you can use to create a slide show presentation that you can show on things like a projector, website, or even email to someone else to view. Plus, you can also print out your slides if you want to have handouts for your audience to review later.

Menu

Edit Menu

The Edit menu does not contain anything new that we haven't seen before in Docs or Sheets.

View Menu

The View menu will allow you to change how your presentation is shown on the screen, which makes it easier to fine-tune and perfects it before showing it to an audience (figure 5.4).

Creating a presentation;

Before we make a plunge, it's imperative to characterize what we mean by 'intelligent introduction.' 'Intelligent' is once in a while used to depict introductions that incorporate test questions or crowd investment – that is not what we're discussing here. At the point when we state 'intelligent,' we're talking about an interactive introduction that utilizes hyperlinks to assist clients with exploring to various areas. An introduction with hyperlinks is 'intuitive' because it permits the client to pick what data they see and request. When in doubt of thumb, a quick introduction functions admirably when your crowd needs to connect legitimately with what's on the screen, placing them in charge of how they digest the data. In this blog entry, we'll stroll through how to make a quick introduction to Google slides.

Specialized viewpoints, bit by bit

Presently that we're in the same spot, how about we dig into how to make a viable intuitive introduction in Google Slides. It's simpler than you may suspect.

Stage 1

Start by opening another introduction! From the Google Slides landing page, look to the upper left, and snap the Blank catch to open another presentation. This is your clear record from which to make an excellent, intelligent introduction!

Stage 2

Google Slides naturally embeds a title slide when you open another introduction, so you should simply tap on the title text box and type in a title. Make the title something bright and snappy, that your crowd can undoubtedly comprehend.

Stage 3

Now, how about we proceed onward to the immensely significant menu slide. We will make something that resembles a catch, so your crowd knows it's interactive. Later on, we'll include hyperlinks. You can utilize any shape for your score, yet rectangular shapes with adjusted corners regularly look the most 'button-like'. Find the Shape button on the toolbar in slides and select a form in the first place. At that point, double tap on the slide, and that shape will show up—Snap and drag utilizing the hubs along the edges of the form to change its size.

This first catch you have made is the reason for your menu. You can do this by reordering. Essentially select the whole catch – click with your mouse and drag over the score, so all components are featured – at that point, reorder it by right-clicking, choosing Copy, and afterward Paste anyway ordinarily you need. Alter the content of each catch to compare to the area of the introduction it will connect to. Next, guarantee that the snaps are adjusted in a type of request. You can choose different fastens and afterward modify or circulate them as you like utilizing the arrangement apparatuses found under the Arrange tab.

Stage 4

Make area header slides for each segment in your introduction. Do this by exploring the head of the page and clicking a new slide on the upper left of the instrument bar. Rehash this progress the same number of times as fundamental. Next, form the same amount of catches as you require for the subsection utilizing the means laid out above. You can likewise essentially reorder the scores you've just made, and simply alter the content.

Stage 5

Add the data you need to remember for each segment. On the off chance that this is pictures, as in our model introduction, at that point, embed photos utilizing the Insert tab.

Suppose this is text, type on the slide utilizing a book box. Be that as it may, it's most suitable to use visuals rather than long passages of text. Keep your message clear and brief.

Stage 6

Rehash stages 4 and 5 for each segment. Ensure each section has a header slide, with catches if vital. Glance through your introduction so far – ensure all the parts are requested accurately, and that there is a header slide toward the start of each.

Stage 7

Come back to your underlying menu slide. Make straightforward shapes to cover each 'button' you have made. We will transform these straightforward shapes into hyperlinks that permit clients to explore through your deck. First, press the Shape button on the toolbar, and afterward make a shape that covers the catch that you have made, however no void area outside them. At that point, select the form and snap the Fill shading button on the toolbar, select Transparent from the drop-down menu.

Spot these straightforward shapes over the head of each catch in your deck. Utilizing direct forms along these lines makes it a lot simpler to alter the hyperlinks if necessary and makes it more uncertain that a client will miss an interactive territory!

Stage 8

Presently we are prepared to hyperlink each fasten! Select the first straightforward box on your menu slide, right snap, at that point, select link, and pick Slides in this introduction. From here, choose the slide you need your catch to explore when clicked.

Tip: If your slide has a title, it will have a similar title in the connection segment, making it simpler to discover. After you have connected these two slides, the connection will remain associated with the particular slide, not the slide number – so it doesn't make a difference if you move things around.

Stage 9

Rehash this procedure for all catches, with the goal that everyone connects to the right slide.

Stage 10

Make catches to come back to the principle menu. To do this, follow the means plot already and utilize a straightforward box that connections back to the principle menu slide. If you include various subsections inside a segment, you can likewise make a catch connecting back to the area title slide from every paragraph.

Formatting a presentation;

It is now time to take all of the work we have been doing on our presentation and make it look a little better, so it doesn't look like it was created in five minutes. This is where formatting comes into play. There are several ways to format a presentation to make it look more professional. Still, the key is not to overdo it and make it look like you wanted to try every formatting option available.

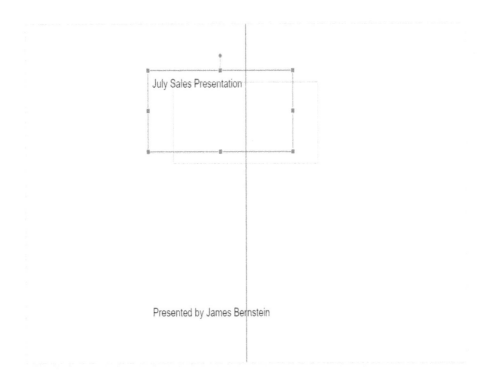

An easier way (in my opinion) is to make the text box the entire width of the slide and then center the text within the text box using the **Align** button on the toolbar, or the **Align and indent** option from the **Format** menu.

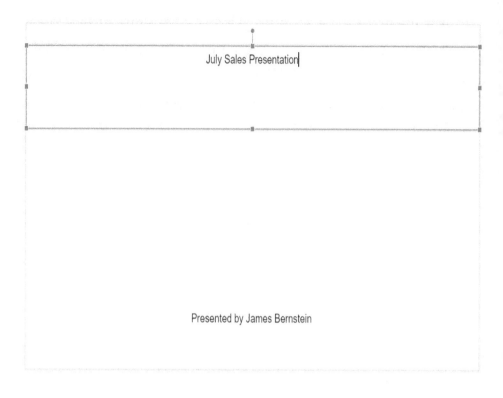

Adding commenters on google slides;

There is also an option to add people and users as commenters. It is a special case of collaboration in which the users added as Commenter will be able to view the file and all the modifications made, but they won't be able to make changes on their own.

This special setting is known as allowing users as "commenter". As they can view the file so they can leave their comments related to the specific content of the shared file. For making this kind of setting, you will follow all the steps which were followed by adding a person as editor.

However, the change will occur after the email address option in which rather than clicking on the can "can edit" option, you will click on the "can comment" option.

In the end, you will click on "Share and save". The commenter, in this case, will also get an email with the notion that the original user wants the commenter to review the file and make comments.

When you are finished with the settings of sharing, you can give it a final touch by verifying the list containing the names of all those people to whom you have allowed the access of the document with specific modifications.

Here there is a crucial aspect of document sharing, which needs to be considered very well. According to this aspect, when an original user gives the other user the rights of the editor, then the editor can also add users as a collaborator.

This greater control and countless utility make Google Drive the only storage Cloud with so much enhanced competence and efficiency. Surely it is an attraction enabling an increase in the number of users.

Printing and share presentation

Google Slides is a free program that is a piece of Google's set-up of online applications, including Google Docs (word handling), Sheets (spreadsheets), Slides (introductions) and Forms (gathering and sorting out data). What's especially incredible about Google Slides is that you can make, alter, team up and present consistently across working frameworks and without potential document similarity or contamination issues, overseeing streak drives or making sense of connector links. Utilizing an automated program likewise disposes of the danger of moving an infection.

Likewise, it is genuinely simple to move an introduction from PowerPoint to Google Slides and back once more; however, you may lose some designing simultaneously. If you do run a presentation, page through to ensure the slides despite everything look how you need them to. Be that as it may, all the substance should change over fine and dandy if you are utilized to PowerPoint and end up expecting to use Google Slides (or the other way around), dread not! The orders and techniques are comparable among them, and on the off chance that you stall out, there are heaps of acceptable online assets to respond to your inquiries

Chapter 6: Google calendar

When you've opened a calendar in your program or on your cell phone, you don't have to do whatever else. It will, as of now, be set up and prepared for use. Both the site and the versatile application have a settings symbol that lets you play with the method that Google Calendar looks and works—and you may likewise need to bring your old schedule into your new one.

Getting Started

Fortunately, you don't have to begin with Google Calendar successfully. For whatever length of time, you have a Google account, and about 1.2 billion individuals do, you don't have to do anything over open calendar.google.com or raise your application. On the off possibility that you've marked into your Google account, you'll as of now be signed in. On the off possibility that you don't yet have a Google account, when you open that page, you'll be welcome to enroll. It's free and doesn't take over a few seconds.

Bringing in Your Calendar

Not many individuals start their schedules with a clear record. On the off possibility that you've been utilizing an alternate schedule application, for example, Outlook or Apple Calendar, you'll have to import your information to Google Calendar. That shouldn't be hard!

In your source schedule, look in the menus for an Export work. Schedule information can take various organizations. CSV is the best with Google Calendar, yet if you're sending out from an Apple Calendar, pick a card. Ensure that you know where you spared the data! In Google Calendar on your PC, click the settings symbol at the upper right. Under Import and fare, pick Import.

Other Calendar Importing Options

That technique ought to be sufficiently clear, and it shouldn't present you with any issues. Be that as it may, if moving from an Apple Calendar to Google Calendar does not go as easily as you would like, there is a subsequent strategy.

First, you'll have to change the default schedule on your iOS gadget to your Google account. Open Settings > Calendar on your iPhone or iPad, and press Default Calendar, pick your Google account. Snap iCloud > Accounts, and slide the catch with the goal that it's in the on position.

The following piece is the place it begins to get fun.

Sign in to iCloud and tap the Calendar symbol. Pick the schedule you wish to fare and snap the communicate logo on the right. You'll see a window checked Calendar Sharing.

Settings

When you've set up your Google Calendar, you can begin playing with the settings. The settings symbol for Google's Calendar site is at the upper right of the screen.

Snap the machine gear-piece, and you'll create a drop-down menu, with the Settings at the head of the rundown. Pick Settings, and on the left of the screen, you'll see a rundown of the entirety of the settings that you can alter in your schedule.

Language and Region

A portion of those settings is direct. Google will set the Language and area dependent on the data it gathers naturally from your Internet association; however, you can transform them if you need to utilize a language and locale that is not the same as your immediate area.

<u>Time Region</u>

The equivalent is valid for your Time zone, yet this is somewhat more mind-boggling. Make an occasion, and Google will naturally utilize your neighborhood time. Welcome another person to join that occasion, and they'll see it in their neighborhood time as well.

So on the off possibility that you were writing in your schedule in New York that you needed to put a call to somebody in California, you may consider them to be of the call at 11 a.m.; however, your partner would think it to be 8 a.m. As you travel, the occasions utilized by your schedule conform to the neighborhood time region.

That change ought to happen naturally. Google will change its time region dependent on your IP address or your phone information. No matter how it might be, on the off chance that it doesn't occur—if you're utilizing a VPN, for instance, or not associated with the Internet—you can likewise show several time region settings in your schedule place you happen to be. You can change your schedule's time region settings physically.

To show more than one-time region setting on the schedule, open Settings, pick a time zone and check Display secondary time region.

What's more, if you're utilizing many schedules, a component we'll talk about later, you can once in a while make distinctive time regions for each schedule. Snap the schedule in the Settings; at that point, select Calendar Setting and change the time region. Few out of every odd schedule permits that change, yet it very well may be a helpful method to monitor another person's occasions in another time region.

Editing Your Calendar

Presently, you've made your schedule. It's set up how you need it. You've included numerous various calendars. What's more, you've imparted a portion of those calendars to companions, associates, or family. Presently you get the opportunity to put sections into that schedule. There are heaps of various approaches to do that—and more than one sort of passage.

Instructions to Add an Event

Make occasion on google schedule site

You can include occasions both from the schedule site and from the application. What you can do on every one of those, stages; however, is marginally unique.

There are two different ways to make an occasion on the site.

You can tap on the in addition to the symbol at the base right of the page to see the full occasion creation structure.

Or on the other, hand you can tap out on the town, which will produce a smaller than expected structure, welcoming you to fill in the occasion's most significant subtleties.

Include Event Form

At the head of the layout is the guidance to Add title and time.

Make google schedule occasion structure

All you type, there is the title. This is the thing that you'll find in the schedule—and recall that in case you're making more than one throughout the day occasion around the same time, those titles will be orchestrated in a subsequent request.

Next, you can pick between making an occasion or an update. We'll return to updates later; however, the default setting is to create an occasion. You, at that, point get the opportunity to enter a date. Since you tapped on a day to raise the structure, the default setting is that the occasion will last the entire day and will just happen on that day. Snap-on one of those dates, however, and Google will offer a month to month plan that permits you to enter several days. That single day occasion can turn into seven days in length happening, for example, a get-away or a gathering.

Different Options

On the off possibility that it's not occurring throughout the day, you'll likewise need to enter a beginning and end time by clicking Add Time.

Finally, if you've made different schedules, you can pick the schedule you need to utilize. That is significant and barely noticeable. Pick an inappropriate schedule, and anybody you're imparting that schedule won't have the option to see the occasion. Snap Save, and you'll be finished. The occasion will be on the schedule.

In any case, you can accomplish more. Press the More Options interface close to the Save catch, and you'll be taken to a nitty-gritty structure with a vast amount of various choices. A large portion of them is apparent; however, some interest a little idea.

• Add Complete Event Form

• After the title and the time is a choice to change the Time Zone.

Google Schedule Make the Event Site Structure

This isn't something that you're going to require frequently; however, it may be valuable if the occasion will occur in an alternate time region. You can even begin the occasion in a one-time area and end it in another—relevant if you're physically entering the subtleties of a flight or posting a gathering on a maritime yacht.

Event Details

The following area is increasingly confusing. This is the place you can enter the occasion subtleties. You don't need to do this stuff; however, it tends to be helpful, particularly if you're welcoming others to participate.

Other Event Detail Options

The following alternative is the sort of warning you can get. This is surprisingly convoluted. You can decide to get the notice by email or get it as a notice in your program or on your cell phone. You can set to what extent before the occasion you get that notice in minutes, hours, days, or weeks, and you can include more warnings just if you—or your visitors—may overlook. In case you're setting up a significant occasion, for example, a wedding, those recurrent warnings sent far out can be helpful.

The territory on the screen's privilege lets you include visitors so they can see it on their schedules and permit them to connect with the occasion in various manners. You can let them change the occasion, welcome others to participate, and see every other person who has been welcomed. Of those three, you'll most likely just need to check the last box.

Chapter 7: Google form

Google Form is free cloud-based application software used to create forms to collect data from users, get

Feedback from the audience and creates a survey or poll among the targeted audience and also to track the attendance performance in an organization.

How to create a form

To create a form, follow the steps below.

Open your Google Drive

Click on "New"

Mouse on "more" from the dropdown menu

Select "Google Forms" Select "Blank form" (or "From a template" if you want to use an existing template)

Click on "Untitled form" to name your document

Connecting Forms to Spreadsheet

You can connect a form with a spreadsheet to collect data from users. Thereby use the data collected to generate charts/graphs. To connect your Form with a spreadsheet, follow the steps below:

Open your Google Drive

Double-click on the form file to open it

Click on "Responses"

Click on the "Spreadsheet icon "in the response, as shown above.

You will be prompted to select a response destination. Select "Create a new Spreadsheet."

Select "Create a new spreadsheet."

Click "Create"

Sending out a form and view responses

Review finishing affirmation

Convey the overview

Snap "email this structure" to convey the overview.

Email the connection to the review

Then again, you can convey a connection to the study on Google+.

Offer a review on Google+

View reactions

Review reactions assemble in a spreadsheet spared to your Google Drive. Open the spreadsheet to see the responses.

View reactions in your Google Drive spreadsheet

Alter the review later

Should you have to alter the Google Form then, open the spreadsheet from your Google Drive. Snap-on the "Structure" menu thing and pick "Alter Form." This will help you to return the first screen, which is used to do the review.

More uses for Google Forms

Google Forms can likewise be inserted, which implies you can utilize a Google Form on your site. A site guest could enter their name and data, which would go straightforwardly into the spreadsheet. Or on the other hand, utilize a structure to lead a study after a Google+ Hangout or occasion, since a Google Form can be shared on Google+. Offer the review with the general population or any of your Google+ circles. Google Forms makes online studies essential.

Chapter 8: Google keep

Keep – Keep is used to do things such as take notes, create lists, and also make audio reminders, so you don't forget the things you need to do.

Sharing

Things in your Keep application can be shared legitimately with different clients without experiencing the standard offer menu you may see in various projects. Select a note or picture you wish to share and pick the individual symbol. You will have the choice to include a client's email address or their name from your contacts.

This transforms you both into teammates. Presently at whatever point anybody makes changes to a note, alters will consequently be noticeable all the individuals with whom it is shared; however, the first organizer can renounce access whenever.

Google keep chrome extension

App Launcher

You can use App Launcher to select any of the G Suite applications to be easily displayed in your app square panel. This is especially useful as a teacher, as many of you will get frustrated with Google Classroom not being listed in the default apps listed.

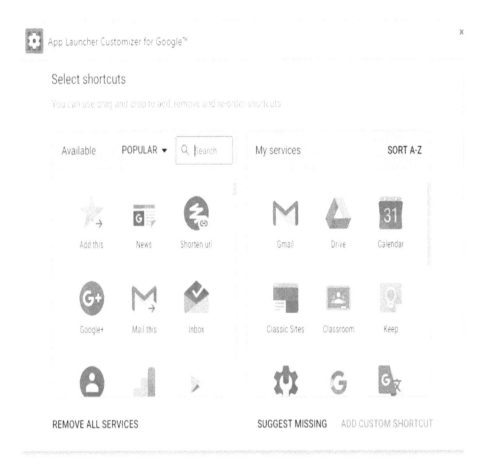

Shown here is the menu where you customize the apps you want to be displayed from a list of commonly used apps.

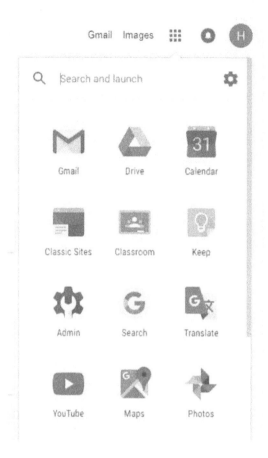

Here is an example of what App Launcher could turn your squares into, and as you can see, it is much more useful this way to what you need.

Facebook   Hotmail   Yahoo

You can also use this extension to create your own custom links to any site you like as shown above here with the Facebook, Hotmail, and Yahoo links.

Share to Classroom

Share to Classroom is definitely going to be a must app for a large number of people, and depending on your G Suite set up in your school could be one of the most useful extensions you have.

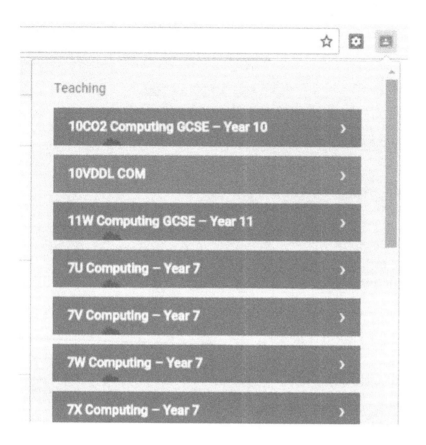

Once selected, you can see all of the possible classes you have access to via Classroom, as shown here in this image.

You can then choose which class you would like to send the link to, and the next screen will give you the different options available for doing it.

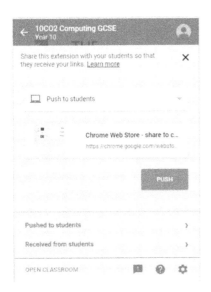

The first option available to you is called 'Push to students, ' which will send the website page to all of the students in your Google Classroom. The website will magically appear in their Chrome browser.

If you do not have Chromebooks, this can still be used, providing all of the students have signed into Chrome on their desktop/laptop and also have the extension installed.

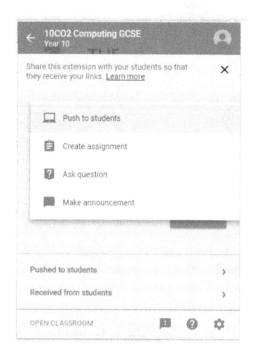

The other options available to you via the drop-down menu are all of the Google Classroom posts you can normally create in Google Classroom.

If you use this drop-down, you can choose the type of post you would like to create, and Share to Classroom will include the link to the page you were looking at automatically.

Screencastify

This extension has proved useful to me in so many ways, from recording technical training for people on using specific ICT tools to providing students with feedback. Screencastify is essentially a screen capture piece of software; however, being a Chrome Extension, its functionality is built into your browser. You can use Screencastify to record anything you would like to demonstrate, and it will record and store in Google Drive all of the video files.

Screencastify can also be used to provide really quick visual feedback to students. You can record looking at a student's piece of work and quickly dictate what the problems and improvements required would be (just like in a lesson!) and then send the video to the student. You can also use some of the inbuilt tools to highlight areas or circle areas on screen in your videos as well. Screencastify can make use of your webcam, and you can record yourself giving the instructions or explanation.

Mote

This is a relatively new Chrome extension; however, in my mind, a precious and useful one. Mote allows you to leave voice comments on your Google Doc in a matter of seconds. It is designed to work perfectly with Google Doc comments. It, therefore, is faster to use than some other options available such as Screencastify, which could achieve a similar goal of leaving voice comments for your students.

Here is a comment

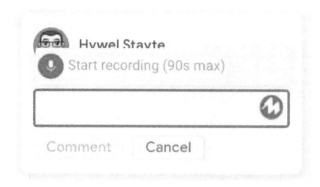

When you leave a comment on a Google Doc, you now get the Mote icon on the right-hand side of the comment box. Click on this button to record your voice comment.

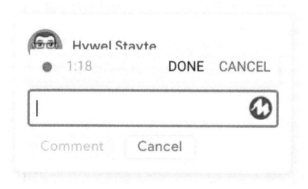

While recording, you are given an on-screen timer so you know how much of the 90 seconds allowed you have left to go, and you can press Done once you are finished.

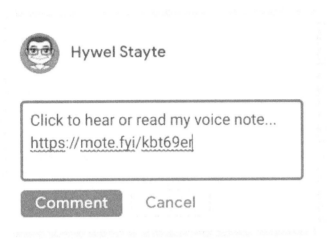

The default message is put in here, which you can then post or use the link to listen to on the Mote website. After you press comment, Mote will transcribe the audio into text and post that with the

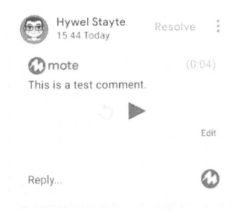

comment as well as the audio.

Here you can see the transcribed comment and the button to play the audio. Sometimes the translation is not perfect, but you have an easy edit button so you can adjust what is written as shown in the images below.

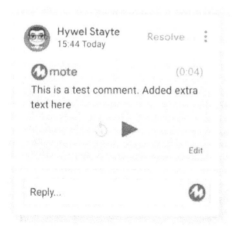

Draft back

This can be a very useful extension that will load and activate automatically whenever you are on a Google Doc. Draft back uses all of the revision history to produce a video of all of the edits and shows you a very cool progression.

Along with these benefits mentioned above, it is also very cool to watch a document's creation with all the edits and revisions that go into it!

Save to Drive

You can use this extension to save web content or screen capture directly to Google Drive. Simply click on the icon listed in the extension area, and your default settings will be used to capture to your Google Drive.

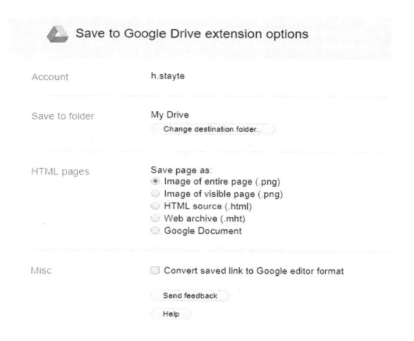

These options can be set up in advance to be your preferred settings when using Save to Drive so that you can use the extension quickly and efficiently.

Random Student Generator for Google Classroom

This is a great little extension to have in the classroom and allows you to very quickly randomly select a student from your classroom. The way the extension works is it is integrated with your Google Classroom, meaning that all the names of your students are already populated into the extension.

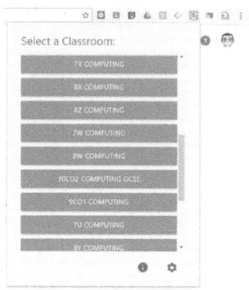

Once you select the extension from the menu, you can choose from all your Google Classrooms available. Upon choosing the class automatically, a random student will be selected and displayed in a pop-out web page window.

Chapter 9: Google photos

Google Photos is a device that can store photographs, recordings, and screen captures taken by your telephone.

It's a strong media reinforcement to have available to you. Furthermore, because it's a cloud-based device, it can let loose space on your telephone. Also, it takes a shot at both Android and iOS gadgets.

How accomplished Google Photos work?

Google Photos clients can transfer new photographs, see, alter, spare, and make original recordings, liveliness, and arrangements, collections, and photographs books. You can likewise download everything, which means your cloud-based reinforcement would itself be able to be effortlessly sponsored up onto your PC or external hard drive.

You can likewise set your Google Drive to keep a duplicate of your photographs and recordings by heading off to your drive's settings, turning on "Make a Google Photos Folder," and clicking save. As pictures are added to your record, they will be arranged into classifications.

Google Photos accompanies free, limitless capacity — yet that is just if you select to spare "top-notch" pictures rather than unique quality pictures, which may be a higher goal. That implies those more essential documents will be compacted to save space, except if your record's settings state in any case. As far as possible for photographs is 16MP, while recordings are compacted to 1080p.

You can permit auto-pressure for future transfers by heading off to your settings and choosing "high caliber." Furthermore, you can apply that change to past photographs by clicking "recuperate capacity," which is additionally situated inside settings.

For the individuals who want to go with unique document measures, it's free up to 15GB, and that incorporates everything from Photos to Gmail to everything else in the drive. From that point forward, you could overhaul through the Google One membership plan, beginning at $1.99 every month for 100GB.

Interfaces:

The Google Photos interface is pretty simple and easy to figure out once you've used it for a little while. It will organize your photos by date and group them, so they are in chronological order. If you want to have specific types of pictures grouped together, then you can create albums to accomplish that. There is also an option to create a photo book that you can send to another person for them to view.

The strong hunt alternative is a significant draw for the stage. It lets you look for normal subjects, similar to "canines" or "seashore" to limit your choices, which is particularly helpful because you haven't yet arranged your photos into collections.

Google Photos is a ground-breaking and adaptable instrument that requires little exertion to use to its fullest. Also, given the way that it gives free, boundless capacity without relinquishing a lot on the photograph and video quality, it tends to be a strong alternative for sponsorship up your media documents.

Adding Photos

There are a couple of ways you can add pictures to your Photos account. One way is to click on the **Upload** button at the top of the page and then browse for the files you want to add.

+ Create   ⬆ Upload

Another way is to just drag and drop pictures from your computer right into the Photos browser window.

You can also click on the **Create** button and start with a new album, photo book, or one of the other options to start organizing your photos and videos as you upload them.

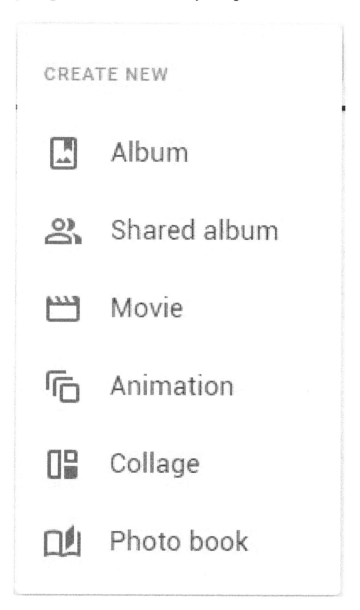

You have a couple of choices when you upload pictures to your Photos account. If you choose to let Google decide the quality of your pictures, then it won't count against your storage limit. But if you want to keep your pictures at a really high resolution, then

Upload size

Choose how you want to upload photos & videos. Your preference is saved in settings. Get help deciding

◉ High quality (free unlimited storage)
Great visual quality at reduced file size

◯ Original (12.2 GB left)
Full resolution that counts against your quota

Continue

it will count against your total available space (which is fine unless you are getting **low** on space).

After the picture is uploaded, Photos will give you an option to add it to an album or to a shared album, which is nice if you are organizing your pictures as you are uploading them. If you don't want to add it to an album, then simply click on the X

After your image is uploaded, it will be marked with the date and location if the picture itself has been tagged. This will happen with uploaded videos, as well (figure 8.8).

Sat, Sep 1, 2018 McKe...

Creating Albums

Albums are used to organize your photos and videos, just like you would with a physical photo album for your "old school" printed pictures. Photos will create some albums of its own when you have a bunch of uncategorized pictures uploaded.

To create a new album, simply click on the **Create album** button to begin the process.

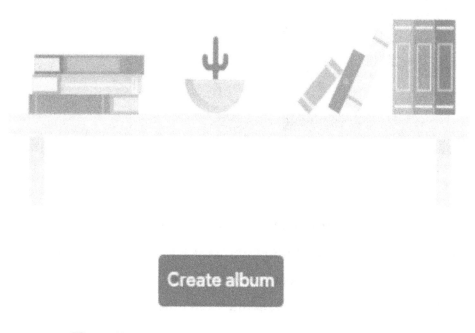

The albums you create are shown here

You will then be prompted to add a title to the album and then some photos. You can choose from your pictures that you have already uploaded, or you can click on **Select from the computer** to upload new ones to your new album. There is also an option to search for photos if you have a lot, and it's hard to find what you're looking for being ready to view.

You will be prompted to share your new album with family and friends if you choose to do so, but this step is optional.

There will be three buttons at the top right of your album that you can use to perform various functions.

Add photos – If you would like to add more pictures to this album, you can do so by clicking the **Add photos** button.

Share – This option will allow you to share the album with people in your contacts or others by adding their email address. There is also an option to share your album to Facebook and Twitter if you have one of those social media accounts. Finally, you can create a link that you can copy and paste into an email and send it off to

Slideshow

Download all

Edit album

Options

Set album cover

Create photo book

Delete album

someone. Then the person you shared the link with will be able to see the pictures and videos within your album, but not any of your other pictures or videos.

Here you have many choices in changing how your album looks, plus some other options.

Slideshow – This will run a full-screen slideshow presentation of all the pictures within the album.

Download all – Choosing **Download all** will let you download all of the pictures in the album to your local device.

Edit album – If you want to rename your album or change the orders of the pictures, then you can do so from here.

Options – This will let you turn the sharing of the album with anyone who has the shared link on or off.

Set album cover – If you want to choose a different default photo for the album cover, then you can do so from here.

Delete album – Finally, if you do not want the album anymore, you can delete it here. It will not delete the actual pictures, but only the album.

Photo Books

Photo Books is a service from Google where you can choose pictures from your storage images and have custom photo books printed out and sent to you. These are not free, of course, and start at $9.99 and go up depending on how many

Pictures you use, the number of pages, and if you want hardcover or softcover. Think of them as Albums that you can have printed out in a custom book format.

When you go to **Photo Book** in Google Photos, you will see some suggestions as to what kind of books you can create, and Photos will try and select pictures from your collection to match that category.

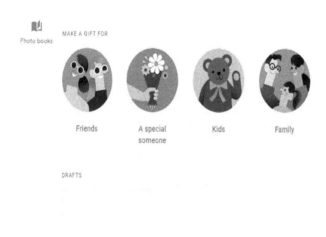

If you see the message, that means that you don't have face grouping enabled in your settings (settings will be discussed later). Face grouping is used by Photos to "tag" faces so it can help to organize the people in your photos.

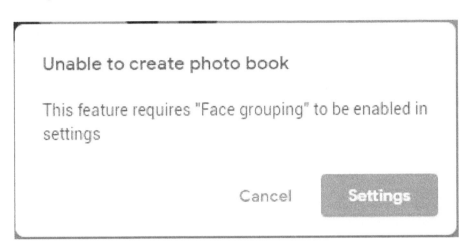

This just means that you didn't tag any people in your photos when you uploaded them, but you can do that after the fact if you wish. That way, when you search for someone, it will bring up the results based on who or what or where you are searching for.

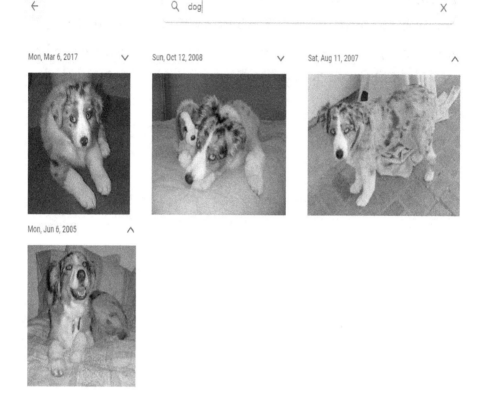

Getting back to Photo Books, once you start a new one, you can choose any pictures from your account. Then when you are done, you can organize them the way you like by dragging them around your screen. The first picture will be the title image, and you can add some text for the title as well

When you are satisfied with your image selection and layout, you can choose the Checkout button and Photos will give you the cost of your picture book based on how many images you have and what type of book you want to have created.

137

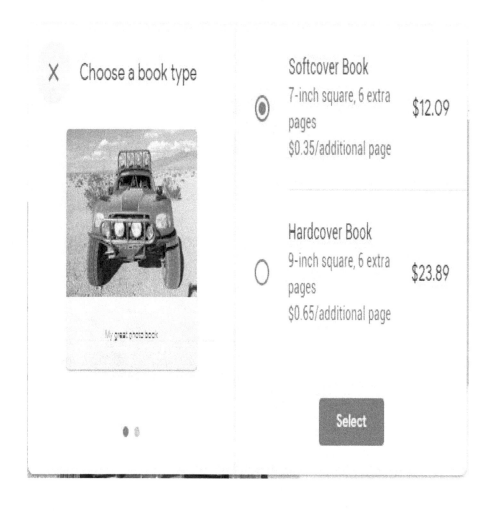

X Choose a book type

Softcover Book

7-inch square, 6 extra pages

$0.35/additional page

$12.09

Hardcover Book

9-inch square, 6 extra pages

$0.65/additional page

$23.89

Select

My great photo book

Then you can go through the checkout process, make your payment, and wait for your photo book to arrive. If you want to save it to edit or purchase later, you can save it as a draft, and it will then show up under the **Drafts** section of Photo Books

Photo books

MAKE A GIFT FOR

| Friends | A special someone | Kids | Family |

DRAFTS

My great photo book

Start a new book

My great photo book

Feb 13, 2019 · Edited Today

Sharing;

Just like with all the other apps, sharing is a big part of the Google experience, and that is no different for Photos. Plus, I'm sure you know how much people love to share their photos anyway.

When you go to the Sharing section in Photos, it will show you your shared photos and videos (if you have any). It will also show you any albums that have been shared with you by other people.

If you want to get rid of albums that have been shared with you, then you can click on the three vertical dots on the album image and choose **Leave album**. There is also an option to block the user who is sharing photos with you as well as report abuse in case you end up with a photo stalker!

For any albums that you created, you will have the option to delete them, which will remove photos added by the other user(s) and prevent them from accessing your photos and videos that you have shared.

Delete shared album?

Deleting this album will:

- Permanently remove any photos added by others
- Stop others from accessing your photos

Your own photos & videos remain safe in your library

Cancel   **Delete**

To create a shared album, simply click on **Start a new share.** Then you will need to give the album a title and choose which photos and\or videos you want to be included in this album. Once you have made your selections click on the **Done** button. Then you can review your album and will have the option to click on **Share** to start the sharing process. If you don't want to share it right away, you can always perform this step later.

X   Review album   Share

Cinder

Jun 6, 2005–Mar 6, 2017 · Shared

If the name is not in your contacts, then you can just type in the email address of the person you want to share with. When you are done, simply click on the send arrow and that's it!

To   todd|

Search results

 Todd Simms
Google Photos

 Todd Simms
tsimms0000@gmail.com

Afterward, you will see all the people that you have shared the album with and be able to add additional people by clicking the + button.

Cinder

Jun 6, 2005–Mar 6, 2017

When you go back to the main sharing area, you will now see your new shared album, along with any other shared albums you might have.

When the person you shared the album with logs into their Google Photos account, they will then see the album you have shared with them.

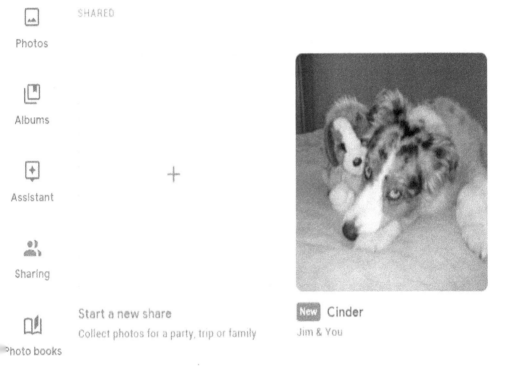

You can also share individual pictures or videos with people by selecting them from your photos and then clicking on the share button at the top right of the screen. Then you will share them the same way you share an album, and they will see the specific shared picture within their **Sharing** section alongside any shared albums.

Settings

Google Photos has a Settings area where you can go and adjust various settings to make Photos work the way you want it to work. (Or at least **more** like you want it to work.) The Settings section is located on the main menu on the left of the Photos interface

○ High quality (free unlimited storage)
Great visual quality at reduced file size

◉ Original (15 GB left)
Full resolution that counts against your quota

Buy storage

Shared libraries
Automatically share photos with a partner

Assistant cards   ⌄
Select cards you want to see in your Assistant

Group similar faces   ⌄
Manage preferences for face grouping

Sharing   ⌄
Manage preferences for sharing

Draft reminder emails
Photo book draft expiration reminders

Google Drive
Sync photos & videos from Google Drive. Learn more.

Activity log   View
View & remove your comments and messages on shared photos

Unlimited photo storage space if you let Google decide how large your image files are, but if you wanted to keep them at their original (and most likely higher) resolution, then it will count against your storage space.

Compress original items to high quality

Recover 15.6 MB of storage by compressing photos & videos from original to high quality

- Also compresses items uploaded elsewhere on Google, such as Google+, Blogger, & Picasa Web Albums
- Does not affect items uploaded through Google Drive

Learn more

Cancel   Compress

Shared libraries – This option lets you automatically share your photos (and videos) with people of your choosing every time you add more to your Photos library. You can set up this sharing by clicking on **Shared libraries**.

Assistant cards – If you don't think you will have any use for the **Assistant card** feature of Photos, then you can turn off specific parts or the entire thing from here.

Sharing – The **Sharing** options allow you to do things such as enable sharing suggestion notifications and remove location tags from your shared items in case you don't want others seeing that information.

Activity log – When you share photos or albums, others can comment on them and send you messages about them. If you click on **View** in this setting, you can see those comments and messages all in one place.

Chapter 10: Gmail

Gmail is the world's electronic mail service of choice, riding higher than any other web-based email exchange. Since April 1, 2004, when its beta version was launched, this free mail service created by Google LLC, has grown in leaps and bounds, grossing 1.5 billion average monthly users in 2018. This accounted for 21 percent of the global email market. And the growth is far from cooling off.

Google, on its part, has surpassed expectations in meeting the needs of a hugely popular and fast-growing webmail system. Besides the addition of several products and innovations to enhance user satisfaction, the Google Company has made Gmail available in 75 languages, assessable to nearly all internet users on earth.

Free e-mail service

Some 1.5 billion active monthly users as of 2018. And, you expect the number to have grown in 2019.

The average Gmail inbox contained 17,000 electronic messages

• 27 percent of those creating new webmail addresses are doing so on the Gmail platform.

• Among those aged 18 to 29, male or female, 61 percent of them have Gmail addresses, some more than one.

- 92 percent of start-up businesses in the US use Gmail

- In the case of mid-sized companies, 60 percent of them in America use Gmail.

- In all, 54 percent of webmail users aged 30 to 44 years, use Gmail, compared to 23 percent who prefer Yahoo. And how do most people access their Gmail? You can trust it's on hand-held devices. Records show that 75 percent of Gmail users send and receive their emails on mobile devices, mostly on Android and iOS smartphones and tablets.

Signing In and Out of your Google account

If you signed out after creating your Google account, how do you sign in again, when you're ready to use the email system? It's easy.

- Go to gmail.com

- Enter your username

- Also, type in your password

- Click Log in

With a functional Google account, you've got access to a dozen Google services in the digital space. But, since you're interested only in the Gmail service, for now, you can go ahead to download the Gmail app with an orange-colored M icon. You get this free from the Google Play store.

Yea, Gmail is optimized for other notable browsers like Apple's Safari, Window's Internet Explorer, and Firefox. But I've never imagined using anything other than Chrome browser to access it. When you open Gmail on Google Chrome, you get a complete package, as it brings you face to face with other Google products.

With the Gmail app on your home screen or desktop, gaining access to your emails is made easy. You just launch the app, and pronto, your mails are in front of you. Like other webmail services, Gmail has a feature that allows you to import contacts from your phone to populate your email address book.

How to add email contacts

Over time, Gmail will help populate your address book and even help you locate whoever you wish to exchange mails with from your address book. For a start, you've got to build up your address book from your phone contacts.

• On our Gmail home page, click on Google apps

• From the menu of apps that shows up, **select Contacts**

• And from the screen that appears, tap on **Add new contact**

• You should now enter relevant information about the contact in the appropriate spaces

- Tap **Save** to complete

Over time, as you keep sending and receiving emails, Google mail will help you populate your address book, for free. Just as it helps, you call up the names when you need to send them emails, with a slight suggestion from you.

Like all others, the Gmail app comes in different versions, some designed by third-party app developers to support extra features.

Interface

Like all others, the Gmail app comes in different versions, some designed by third-party app developers to support extra features.

While you definitely would prefer the official Gmail app deployed by Google LLC, you should also know that even the official app customizes in three different ways on Android smartphones and tablets; personal computers and laptops; and on iPhone and iPads. Across these devices, you can also view your emails in the HTML mode, if you ever want to do that. The app will display differently in HTML mode.

Sending and receiving emails;

It's time to start sending emails. In this manual, we'd assume you're among the majority of Gmail users who access the webmail on Android mobile devices. Even if you have been doing this for a long while, you can still go through the procedure, if only for the fun of it. Who knows, you may just see a couple of ways to optimize your Gmail user experience.

• On your smartphone or tablet, launch the Gmail mobile app

• Tap the Compose icon represented by a **plus sign (+)** at the bottom of page

• In the **To** space, enter primary recipient of your mail

• If more people need to be in the loop, copy them in the **Cc** space

• You can even blind copy more people in the 'Bcc' field. Your primary recipient and those directly copied, will not be aware you copied those in the Bcc field.

• Then fill in the Subject of your mail

• And proceed to write what you have to tell your mail recipients.

When you're done composing an email, take some moments to read through what you've just written. Read slowly, and pay attention to each word, so you do not read what's on your mind as if it's what you've written down.

If you use Gmail on a PC at school, for work, or in any organizational setup, there's a feature that can automatically fix misspelled words. To autocorrect your mails:

- Click Settings in the top right corner

- Select General

- Enable **Autocorrect**

Each word that's autocorrected will carry a temporary line under it. If you think the correction is inappropriate, you can click undo, to retain the original word, or type in the correct word by yourself. In all, your slogan should be: any unedited text is not worth posting or sending. Unfortunately, sloppy writing seems to be in vogue, with many young adults not giving a damn about spellings and rules of grammar! You don't want to join the millennial carelessness.

Managing email

The navigation of Gmail is simple – reading and writing messages represent the most common user operations, so the focus on making this easy is one of the reasons why Gmail is so popular. But simple doesn't mean basic, and there are many ways to finetune its functionality.

User settings are located in the Settings hyperlink in the top right of the page. Options are split logically into tab groupings, and we will review the key tabs and features here. Depending on whether you are using just Gmail alone or as part of Google Apps, the options will vary slightly.

Since Google frequently adds and changes features and options, these configuration pages are getting ever more numerous and complicated. The upside is that you can really finetune its performance to exactly what you want, though at the expense of finding settings quickly and sometimes having to decipher what they mean.

Managing spam

While there are clear limitations in some of the Google Apps services, since they generally provide only a subset of features of their Microsoft Office equivalents, Gmail is the one application that stands head and shoulders above any other free or paid email software. Gmail combines a fast, intuitive interface that's extremely quick to learn with all the major benefits of working in the cloud: you can store and search gigabytes of messages seamlessly and access your email anywhere.

It also boasts an intelligent spam filtering technology, with many companies reporting a substantial drop in the amount of spam that reaches end-users and simplifying the need for email blacklists and whitelists. Google Apps Premier users can modify the Postini configuration to tweak this spam filter with finer granularity. Additionally, file attachments in email are automatically scanned for viruses - although this can never be completely foolproof, it undoubtedly reduces the number of virus outbreaks on the desktop.

For mobile users, Gmail synchronizes seamlessly with many modern smartphones and is integrated natively into Android devices, with apps available for iPhone and Blackberry. On top of all this, die-hard Microsoft Outlook users are still able to access their email through their preferred client, while taking advantage of Gmail's strengths running on the server-side.

Account settings

There are many tabs or categories for different settings, and each tab has multiple settings underneath it.

Settings

General   Labels   Inbox   Accounts and Import   Filters and Blocked Addresses   Forwarding and POP/IMAP   Add-ons   Chat   Advanced   Offline   Themes

General – These basic settings change the way Gmail looks for the most part. Here are some of the more useful settings:

Images – Having this on or off will allow you to decide if you want images that are embedded (not attachments) into the body of the email to be displayed or not.

Smart Compose – This will give you suggestions for what to say while you are typing, kind of like your smartphone does.

Conversation View – This setting is one you should try out to see which way you like because it makes a big difference when reading emails with multiple back and forth replies. One thing I never liked about Gmail was how these types of emails were hard to sort out because they got too jumbled up when they got too big.

☐	Primary		👥 Social		🏷 Promotions	
☐ ☆ ≫	me, **OCT** 6				**Back and forth message** - My pleasure	
☐ ☆ ≫	Regina, me 15				Fwd: Vet assistance - OK. thanks I was abl	
☐ ☆ ≫	Accounting, me 2				March 2019 Statement	
					📄 Statement177_f...	
☐ ☆ ≫	Google, me, david 3				New Coverage issue detected for site http:	

Then when I open that email, it will show all of the back and forth replies in one place. Which is fine until you start getting into really long conversations, and then things can get a little jumbled.

Smart Reply – Works like Smart Compose, but this time with replies.

Desktop notifications – This will allow Gmail to use popup notifications on your computer when a new email comes in. You can also set it to only notify you when important emails arrive, so you are not bothered by all your incoming emails.

Picture – If you want to have your picture show up in your emails, then you can choose this option. Keep in mind that it will not show up for everyone that you send email to, and mostly to other Gmail users.

Signature – Signatures are used to display information about yourself (such as your title and phone number) at the bottom of the email messages that you send. Vacation responder – This is used to send an automatic reply to any email you get when you are out of town, so you don't have to do it while on vacation, etc. You will type in a default message, and Gmail will reply with that message to your incoming emails.

Turn the Conversation view off, then each email that was addressed to you will be shown separately in your inbox.

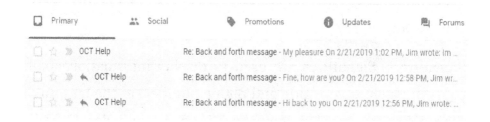

Labels – I have gone over labels in detail, but if you want to customize your labels such as showing, hiding, or removing them, then you can do so from here.

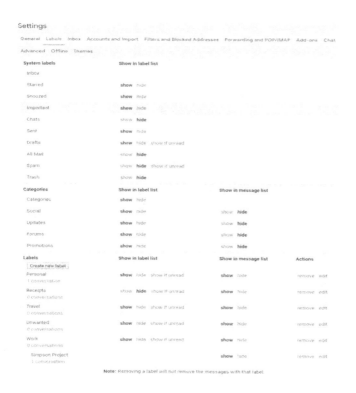

Inbox – These settings only apply to your Inbox, and you can do things such as hide any categories you don't want to be shown and also change settings for Importance markers, which are used to mark emails as important. If you have created any

Accounts and Import – This is where you can make changes to your account, such as your password and setting up recovery options. Recovery options include giving Google your phone number or an alternate email address to be used in case you get locked out of your Gmail account.

Chat – Chat is used to have conversations with other users by using an online messaging format rather than email. Think of it as text on your computer.

Advanced – You most likely won't find yourself changing any options here, but these settings allow you to fine-tune how Gmail works. (Most of the options are disabled by default.)

Offline – Gmail has a feature that will let you do things such as read, respond, and search your email even without an Internet connection. If you respond to an email or compose a new one, then it will automatically be sent once you have your Internet connection back.

Themes – If you want to change the plain and boring look of Gmail, then you can apply a custom theme to your account to spice things up a bit with some images and color.

Chapter 11: Google classroom

Google Classroom was first introduced as something that could be added to G Suite for Education back in 2014 when it was first created, and it was released to the public in August of that year. June of the following year, it was announced that Google Classroom would have a share button that would enable administrators and developers to continue to engage with Google Classroom.

Benefits of google classroom for everyone

The standout benefit of utilizing this software is its ability to save both teachers' and students' time. Using high technology with a comprehensible platform aids the teacher's task, so he or she pays more attention to teaching and achieving the critical focus of the course, rather than having to spend time on small jobs.

Accessibility

Google Classroom allows easy access to course documentation and cloud storage. For teachers, documenting lesson plans is the best way to enable their students to access course content at any time and to be able to study after class as well.

Paperless

This platform also aids transition into a paperless environment as all the tasks will be carried out online. From the teacher uploading lesson notes, assignments, and even assessment tasks to the students completing said assignments, all can be done without having to shuffle an excessive amount of papers.

Time Saver

As has been mentioned earlier, this platform saves a wealth of time. It provides extra time for teachers and students to carry out other tasks because all the materials are stored and accessed in just one particular place.

Also, as all resources are in a specific location, one can access it with any device.

Communication

This learning platform is designed with features for interaction between teachers and students.

Collaborate

This software also creates a forum for collaboration. Students can work together on tasks in Google Docs created by the teacher.

Engagement

Google Classroom provides varying means to enhance learning and make it a more fun venture. It also allows teachers the opportunity to add videos and web pages into lessons.

Differentiation

With Google Classroom, teachers can give out separate tasks to their students. With just a few steps on the Classwork page, teachers can assign lessons to the whole class or specific groups of students.

Feedback

A significant way for students to learn and improve is by getting feedback from their instructors. This software allows for feedback tools for teachers when grading their students.

This software also comes with a comment bank that can be used in the future within the grading tool. Users can also drop notes while using the Classroom mobile application.

Getting started:

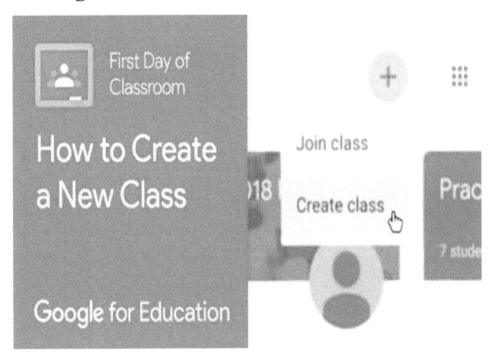

As stated earlier, it starts with opening a Google account. After that, you'll proceed to the Google Classroom page, as depicted in the image.

From the Google Classroom page, click on the (+) button and then select the Create Class option from the drop-down menu. You are expected to click the EULA checkbox and select CONTINUE. A page will pop up.

From that page, you will need to assign a name to your class. You'll also need to specify the section, and the subject you will be discussing.

Giving a Name to Your Class

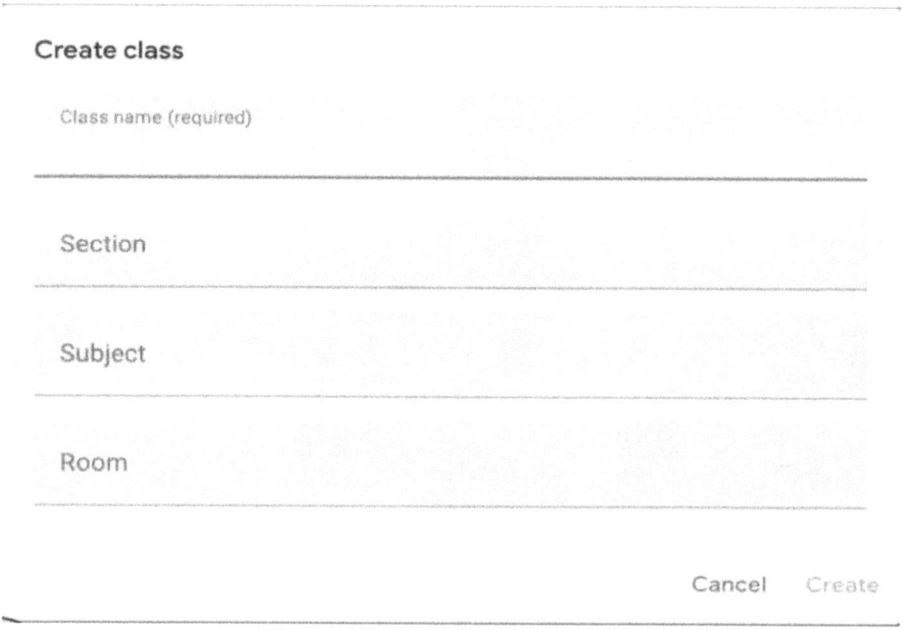

Create class

Class name (required)

Section

Subject

Room

Cancel   Create

After filling out all the information in the picture above, you can then click **create.** And as simple as that, you've created your class! Upon completing this, the next thing is to set up and customize the classroom.

Your class is ready!

You should get a message welcoming you to your class. There are several things to attend to on this page. We'll highlight them all.

For a start, you'll need to select a theme for your class. Click the Select Theme or Upload a Photo option to do this. Once you've picked the perfect look, it's time to write a description for the class.

That can be done by clicking the About tab on the screen and then selecting the option to do that in the next window. The option dots should be clicked. There you'll see the edit options.

Click on it and enter the description for your class. You can add the meeting location and other details, as provided in the image below.

Creating the Class Description

Managing the Class Drive Folder is the next thing to do. The folder is where you will drop all class assignments and materials. You will update them to this folder and make them accessible to all your students. From Google Drive, you would've noticed that sharing permission is only for teachers.

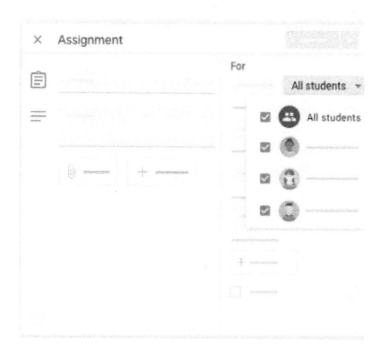

You can't and shouldn't give this permission to students in your class. Students should only be able to access their assignments and materials from this file.

Many prefer creating a subfolder for assignment and material purposes. You can also create a subfolder for teachers where their material will be kept.

Creating a subfolder is very easy, navigate to Google Drive, click on the classroom folder, and open it. You can then select the option to create a new folder inside the classroom folder.

How to Send Invites to Your Students

After setting everything up, you need students in your class. So, sending out invites to them is the next thing.

To do this, click on the student tab and click the invite students' button. If the students are in your Google contacts, you can invite them by name or email address.

So, if you have a list of students, you can send the class link and code to them via email. Upon joining the class, they can start to work on their tasks and interact with other students.

There's no easier way of creating an online class than this method. It's perfectly designed by Google with incredible features that make it perfect for all teachers.

Manage a class;

When you are inside of your Google Classroom, a course is going to represent one "class". It can have any name that the teacher wants, but they will most likely give it a name that will help to distinguish it from the other classes that they are teaching.

The API for Google Classroom will be able to support the class and will include all of the assigned teachers, students, and even the metadata that goes with it. It is also going to be able to support:

Managing the teachers and the students

With the help of the Google Classroom API, it becomes much easier for an administrator to differentiate between the students and the teachers. There may sometimes be when this differentiation can change. For example, there may be one course where a person is considered a student, and another one is a teacher, and then these roles can switch later on.

Once the teacher has access that is needed, they can create a different class for each of the courses that they run. They should make sure that they give them names that help keep things separate if they have several courses that are the same. For example, if they teach three courses of Algebra 1, they may want to name it with the period that they teach each one, like Algebra 1 Period 3 and so on to keep things in order

Once all of the students are in the class, it is so much easier to share information, work on projects together, and so much more. There are so many things that the teacher and the students will be able to work with together inside of Google Classroom, and this area can be perfect whether you are just using this on the side with your regular classroom or if this is going to replace the regular classroom and you are taking everything online. It is so much easier for teachers to provide personalized learning to their students in ways that were just not possible before. With the help of discussions, assignments, and so much more, the student will be able to learn on the Google Classroom and get what they need out of every classroom

How to set due dates

In every course, you share with your teacher and classmates a Classroom calendar and a Google calendar. The admin has disabled the calendar for your class if you don't see calendars.

What would you do for any timetable?

Note: Only computers, not mobile devices, can be used as the classroom calendar.

Classroom calendar for Google

Show due dates of class assignments.

View incidents in class

Add immediate recalls

Add activities, for example.

Sessions of study

Show due dates of class assignments.

To open it, select an object in the schoolroom android phone and iPad computer

See your calendar items.

See the school calendar schedule dates.

You can see the due dates on the Classroom calendar. There are no things you can include.

Go to the the.google.com tutorial.

List Tap

Click the Calendar tab.

Select an option:

Click Back or Next To show the previous or future research past the date.

Tap the file

Click All Classes to view assignments for all your courses.

All classes Click

Select All Classes and pick the class to display assignments for one class.

Click assignment or question to open the classroom. (Optional)

See your Google Calendar for due dates and events.

The due dates and courses, such as field trips or tests, can be viewed on your Google Calendar. You will find all calendars in your Other Calendars folder and choose whether to display or cover them.

Go to the the.google.com tutorial.

Click Classwork.

Click Google Calendar.

Click the Calendar tab.

(Factory) Click the item for information.

Calendar of Google

(Optional) Checkbox for the class to see or hide calendars of other classes at the left, below Other Calendars.

Fill in Google Calendar things.

Please add a personal message.

A notice for remembrance of your calculator, for example, can be added. Everything in the Google Calendar you add does not appear in the Classroom Calendar.

Go to the the.google.com tutorial.

Click Classwork.

Click Google Calendar.

Click the Calendar tab.

Go to Add Recallers for further guidance.

Fill in a case

You can incorporate activities like a study session and invite your fellow students. Everything in the Google Calendar you add does not appear in the Classroom Calendar.

Go to the the.google.com tutorial.

Click Classwork.

Click Google Calendar.

Click the Calendar tab.

Brainstorm – Use Google Docs for class tasks, papers, slides, or sketches.

Due Dates Calendar-Link a Google calendar to the classroom with due dates, tests, and other important dates.

Test homework – The classroom enables the review of homework by looking at the assignment page quickly. If more grading is needed, only have access to the grading interface for the job.

Selection Boards – Choose how students show their skills by setting up an option board and uploading it as a mission. Selection boards allow students to select from different tasks and are accessible directly in classrooms, using Google Docs or via external applications.

Classes for co-teaching – invite others to join in your classroom. Every teacher can create assignments and post announcements for students.

Create questions before a Socratic seminar – create a task before a Socratic seminar that allows students to ask about questions. Students may delete redundant questions during the collaborative process.

Arrest warrant file – Build a Google Docs arrest document. The worksheet can then be shared privately through the classroom with the detention teacher and individual students.

Digital Portfolios – By uploading documents, photos, artifacts, and so on, students can create digital portfolios for their work.

Guidance Guide – Using Google Docs to create classroom guidance papers.

Homework and assignments:

Creating an Assignment in your Google Classroom. The Google Classroom serves the purpose of creating assignments and having them assigned to students.

1. Select the tab 'Classwork'. This tab allows you to access on-going assignments and already submitted ones, and you can also create new assignments.

2. Click on the 'Create' option and then select the 'Assignment.'

option.

There are also other options like Question, Material which are used if you want to ask your students a single question or if you want to simply post an attachment or visuals.

3. You should then title your assignment in the box provided and include descriptions or instructions which are optional.

4. There is a lot of flexibility offered here by the Google Classroom platform while creating your assignments as you have options like the due date (you might also include due time if you want) and how many points the assignment will be marked over.

5. Once you are done with this, you should then select the

'Assign' option found at the top right corner.

All of your assignments are taken by the Google Classroom and are added automatically to your Google Calendar. While still on the

"Classwork' tab, you can select the Google Calendar to have a proper view of your schedule and due dates of your assignments.

Each of these 3 types of interactions has their various importance's, which are highlighted below:

Students can view file: This option should be the suitable one for you if your purpose is to make all your students have access to this file without being able to make changes or modifications to it. This is great when you are attaching study guides and generic handouts which are to be made available to the whole class.

Make a copy for each student: In this option, each document will be duplicated, and there will be a copy of the original that has been created by this option. Hence the student can individually complete the copied document. The original copy is still kept intact as the students do not have access to it. In a situation where you have a document that you quickly need to pass on to the students so that they can start working on it or where they have to fill their answers in the provided blanks, this option is ideal for your use.

Inviting students and teachers to classes;

You can make your Virtual Classroom from your Dashboard or from an exercise page. Simply click, make the classroom, and give your classroom a name.

From that point, you can invite understudies to join your new classroom utilizing one of three techniques.

Email The main technique is to enter a rundown of understudy email addresses. Study.com will send an invitation to the messages you give. This is an incredible alternative if you have a rundown of the email that tends to help or just needs to invite a couple of understudies.

Offer connection. The subsequent choice is to utilize an invitation interface. In the wake of making a classroom on your Dashboard, click include understudies and duplicate the invitation interface you are given. You can post this classroom invitation connect to your learning the executive's framework or email it to your group.

With both of these choices, your understudies can make accounts individually at no expense to them. All they have to give is a name, email address, and a secret word.

Classroom code If your understudies as of now have a record, they can sign in and utilize a class code to join your class. At the point when you make a classroom from your Dashboard, you will get a comparing class code. Your understudies can enter this code on their dashboard.

Best google classroom extension;

Google Cast for Education

This is a Chrome app that lets students and tutors share screens wirelessly. With this app, teachers can control who can be added to view the screens and add students from Google Classroom.

Alice Keeler's Classroom Split

This is an extension by Alice Keeler that splits the Chrome screen and allows students to view assignment instructions and work on the assignment side by side. That way, they do not need to keep on shuttling between tabs or minimizing and maximizing constantly.

Google Classroom Apps

Several Apps that integrate with Google Classroom do so through the **Share** button. While some of these apps connect seamlessly for free, you may have to pay to integrate some.

Top useful apps for google classroom;

Aeries: Aeries is an educational app that helps foster learning online. You can integrate your Aeries classes with Google Classroom. You can even import scores from your Google Classroom into the Aeries.

Aladdin: Just like Aeries, Aladdin helps manage to learn online. Aladdin helps with education management. With an Aladdin integration, Google Classroom classed can be automatically created based on classes already created by the teacher on Aladdin.

Alma: Alma is a Student Information System. Alma can integrate with Google Classroom, and teachers can sync assignments across platforms.

Curiosity: Curiosity is an app that brings new knowledge to millions of users to inspire and unleash curiosity. You can easily share content from Curiosity to Google classroom.

Discovery Education: Discovery Education helps tutors and students learn better and provide awesome learning materials. You can integrate their platform with Google Classroom and use both applications side by side.

Pear Deck: This app allows you to connect all the devices in the class for an interactive lesson. The app does away with the need for codes and URLs. It provides a quick, hassle-free connection.

Plagiarism Check: This is a very efficient tool that helps teachers and students look out for similarity between texts. It also helps teachers automate their assessment of writing. It easily alerts the teacher of word substitutions, synonyms, and rearrangements.

Workbench: With Workbench, a project-based learning model is applied. Teachers use tools available on the app to create and track projects which are assigned to students. It also makes use of block-based programming tools to make coding open to users with little coding experience.

Google classroom tips and tricks.

Pick one email for all of your classes

Consider having a dedicated email that is for all of your classes. You don't need to separate it and have an email for each of your classes but create a new email that will only accept information from all classes using Google Classroom. Whenever a teacher announces they use this platform, you will use this email. This helps you to keep all of your classes in one place and can prevent you from missing out on your announcements and assignments because they got lost in all your personal emails.

Check your classes daily

As the year goes on, your teacher will probably get into a routine of when they make posts, and you can check the class at that time. But it is still a good idea to stay on top of a class and check it each day. You never know when you may forget about an assignment that is almost due or when the teacher will add an extra announcement for the whole class.

Look at the calendar

One of the first places you should go when opening up to a class is the Calendar. This is going to list everything important that is coming your way in the next few months (updated as the teacher adds new announcements and assignments) so you can plan out your time. For some students, it is easier to get a grasp on the work when it is in table form rather than just looking at a date in the announcements.

Ask questions for clarification

The classroom makes it easier for students to ask the questions they need before starting an assignment. In some classrooms, it can be hard to find time to ask a question. When twenty or more students are asking questions at the same time, or the teacher runs out of time and barely gets the assignment out before the next bell, there are many students who may leave the classroom without any clue how to begin on an assignment.

Learn all the ways to give feedback.

Your students are going to thrive with as much feedback as you can provide them, and Classroom offers you many options for this. You can leave comments on assignments that students hand in, on the file that is submitted, through email, and so much more. Consider the best places to leave feedback and let your students know so they can be on the lookout for ways to improve.

Use the description feature

When creating an assignment, make sure to add a nice long description. This is where you explain what the assignment is all about, how to complete it, and even when the assignment is due. Often students are juggling many classes all at once, and by the time they get to the assignment, they have forgotten all the instructions you gave them in class. Or if a student missed class that day, the description can help them understand what they missed. A good description can help to limit emails with questions and can help students get started on the assignment without confusion.

Share your links and resources

There may be times that you find an interesting document, video, or other media that you would like your students to see. Or they may need resources for an upcoming project, and you want to make it easier for them to find. In this case, you should use the announcement feature. This allows all the important documents to be listed right at the top of the classroom rather than potentially getting lost further down in assignments.

Chapter 12: Google G Suite

G-Suite Application is a service that provides a suite of cloud Computing, Software, and Products of Google Cloud, productivity, and collaboration of tools. G-Suite provides Services like Gmail, Hangouts, Calendar, and Communication, drive for Storage, Documents, Google Spreadsheets, Google Slides, Google keeps, Google Forms, and Sites of Productivity in marketplace and collaboration and depending on the plan. Google provides the app development platform for app makers.

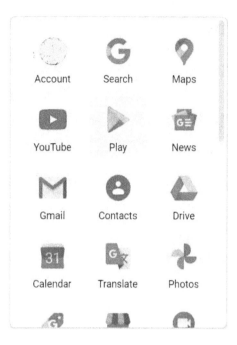

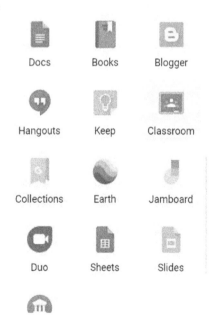

G-Suite Family Comprises there family members like a Gmail, Maps, YouTube, Play Store , News , Hangouts , Meets , Calendar And Google Drive.

Advantages of G-Suite

Get a Business Account Email Free. Improve the Team Collaboration. Provide the Data Security. Unlimited Storage Space provided like Cloud Storage.

Cost Savings.

Disadvantages Of G-Suite

G Suite is a Entirely Web based with no options for Software. If you are using Microsoft Office Service like to you find out that Google Docs and Sheets are not as Powerful.

G Suite Storage less as a compare with Office 365.

Office 365 is still reaching the enterprise market and G Suite still playing Catch Up for grow.

G-Suite family

<u>Gmail</u>

Gmail is very popular Web-based Email Service Platform. It has become a huge platform for many users to perform a Email Service Threaded Database Storage Operation and Conversations between random users and robust Search capabilities.

Gmail is Free Webservice or email service implemented by a Google. Any Users can access Gmail on the internet and Gmail also used for Third Party Synchronize the mail information by forwarded POP and IMAP set of regulations. Gmail is a Main Application of G-Suite Family. Gmail is one type best storage application.....Gmail Provide the best and best facility to their users. Gmail is Available in different 105 languages. Gmail is active for user at anywhere anytime and any places.....its called pocket storage.

Maps

Maps is a Web Mapping Service Provided by Google under the Suite Family. Maps shows to the Satellite image of Earth, Different aerial Photographs, City Maps, 360 view images of City Maps. It also shows the Real time traffic conditions, routing views of Car, Bicycle and Different Public Transformation.

Google Drive

Google Drive is a Storage Service device application that store the various files on cloud and access them from your Computer and Smartphone. In Google Drive you can store the documents, images, videos and backup of your computer and laptop information data. Google Drive is a free storage device to provide the different services.

YouTube

YouTube is Google Platform Service used for Video Sharing that allows to the users to watch a video published by other users and Upload their Videos of their own creativity. It is platform to show your talent and Creativity.

Google Classroom

Google Classroom, Google provides different services like Google docs, Gmail and Google Calendar. Google Classroom is one of the Best services to google provided. Google Classroom saves time and paper and make it easy to create a class, share their notes, assignments and learning Videos and Communicate with each other. Every App has a primary goal like that Google Classroom has the main goal is to process of sharing files between students and teachers.

Many of the colleagues and Schools use this app for the Students to start the new process learn from home.

Play Store:

Play Store is a GSuite family Application. PlayStore is Preinstalled app Store on Android Devices. PlayStore Provides access to content on the store like Apps, Books, Magazine, Music, Movies and Television Programs.

News

Google News is a Computer system which created the News Site that aggregates headlines from advance platform of Worldwide, groups of similar stories together.

Hangouts

Hangouts is a Communication Software design by a Google. It allows users to initialize and participate in text, voice or video chats and Communicate between one on one Groups.

Blog

Blogger is one of the best platforms to show and spread their knowledge to each and every person. Using blog, you can easily express your feelings and technical knowledge. In upcoming era, Blog are most essential way to reader...for complete their reading hungriness.

If you are good writer, Author then you must create your account on the Blog. Publish your passion your way. Weather you did like to share your concepts, experience and Advanced news, create a unique and beautiful blog for free.

My business

Google MyBusiness is free and easy to use an application for businesses and organizations to handle their online presence whole google, including G-Suite applications like Google Search and Google Maps. Google MyBusiness helps to verify and create your business information; you can both help to connect with new customers and show your business to online.

Marketplace

The G-Suite Functionality Application provided by a Google Apps Marketplace. Google Marketplace is an online store application to related Business-oriented cloud applications that argument provided by G-Suite Functionality. Google Marketplace is an

Administrative cloud-based application browse, purchase, and deploy integrated cloud applications.

Jamboard

Google Platform Service provided by one of the best applications is Google JamBoard. Google JamBoard is developed by Google G-suite Family application. It is type of an interactive whiteboard. Google JamBoard has a basically 55"4k TouchScreen Display and it has online interconnection through cross platform system. Google JamBoard can used by two various methods.

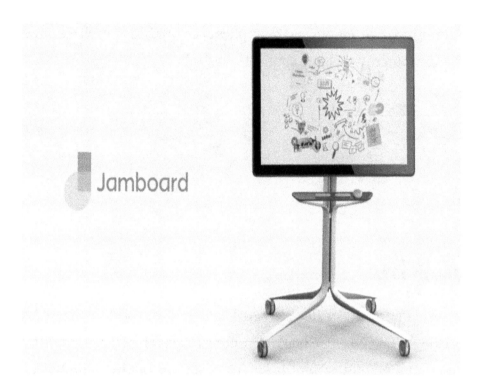

Jamboard

Hangout

Google Hangout is one of the best platforms for connect with people. You can also touch with single person or group. This application is easily accessible on the google play store. You can download in smartphone or computer

The current generation are attracted toward the new technology and they accept the advance concept. They also enjoy the online meets for example, using this application you do video call or voice call to your friends.

Duo

Duo is the special application and plays important role in the Gsuite family. Google Duo is advance and easy to use video calling application. Using this application, you can easily call your friends and loved once.it is one of the best high-quality videos calling application.

Conclusion

Now that you have read through this book and taken your Google Apps skills to the next level, you might be wondering what you should do next. Well, that depends on where you want to go. Are you happy with what you have learned, or do you want to further your knowledge on Google Apps, or maybe even get into the more advanced Google G Suite?

All organizations need to cover their everyday exercises in office organization with a solitary arrangement of office instruments. Having the option to hide these are the primary advantages of utilizing Google Apps (G Suit). With G Suite, Google gives organizations a cloud answer for their everyday work. It has numerous applications that cooperate to cover the entirety of the daily exercises in office organization. The charging of administrations is client dependent on a membership model, from fundamental capacities to increasingly extra highlights.

Google G Suite segments incorporate interchanges applications like Gmail or Google Hangouts, arranging board applications like Google Calendar, cooperation, and distributed storage applications like Google Drive or Google Sites, and requests for Office utilize like Google Sheets, Google Docs or Google Slides.

The best advantage of utilizing Google applications (G Suit) is that organizations needn't bother with their framework to send requests. The applications can be used through an online association from any gadget and area.

Past supplanting capacities gave by another programming; Google Apps offers particular highlights intended to change and improve office working.

If you **do** want to expand your knowledge (or even get into G Suite), then you can look for some more advanced books, or ones that cover a specific technology that interests you. Focus on one subject at a time, then apply what you have learned to the next subject. You can even sign up for a free G Suite trial to see if it's something you want to pursue.

There are many great video resources as well, such as Pluralsight or CBT Nuggets, which offer online subscriptions to training videos of every type imaginable. YouTube is also a great source for training videos if you know what to search for.

If you are content in being a standalone power user that knows more than your friends, then just keep on reading up on the technologies you want to learn, and you will soon become your friends and families go-to computer person.

All together for cloud administrations to agree to European information insurance prerequisites, EU clients can utilize Google to conclude their own EU model agreement provisos and information preparing additional items. Applications like Gmail have worked in spam blockers and infection scanners. Google Drive transferred information is encoded. Dissimilar to Google's free application contributions, clients' data isn't checked and assessed for a limited time. Thus, it is demonstrated that google applications give the best of the highlights in it, which are prescribed to each client for routine utilization.

Giving them a short, exhaustive, and a supportive viewpoint to progressively safe perusing and routine utilization.

CPSIA information can be obtained
at www.ICGtesting.com
Printed in the USA
LVHW021053160221
679322LV00011B/460